1

FACE TO FACE WITH THE GLOBAL ECONOMY

Leo Cecchini

Mallorca, Sept 2019

FACE TO FACE WITH THE GLOBAL ECONOMY

I consider my personal contribution to the world has been to spend my life as a participant in, and builder of, the global economy. Leo Cecchini

INTRODUCTION

The global economy, a phrase that conjures up an image of a unified world, the long hoped for "One World," albeit only in economic terms. As such it commands the attention of all since it reaches the most remote ends of the earth. I do not speak here about total world output gained by adding up all the national economies, but rather the complex structure of interconnections, relations, commerce, finance, and agreements that bring these economies together. National economies fill fixed spaces, the global economy fills the spaces between.

What makes up this singular phenomenon? What are its parts? What are its mechanisms? How does it function? The global economy is not the product of some unified agreement nor even understanding. Rather it is an organic structure that has grown through millions of economic exchanges between the various national economies. Like Topsy, "it just growed."

COMPONENTS

INTERNATIONAL TRADE

The most common topic covered under the title "The Global Economy," is international trade. I became intimately involved in this in both my careers as a diplomat and subsequent time in private business. I know all the steps in international trade from negotiating trade agreements between nations to how to set up secure payment for goods sent from one country to another. The main problem with international trade, as opposed to domestic trade, is that, in the international setting, one does not have recourse to rules and laws to guarantee delivery and payment. As I used to tell those who consulted with me as a government official or as a business colleague, there is only one thing that really matters in concluding a good export/import deal, how well do you know your supplier or recipient? In domestic trade, if someone fails to deliver or pay, you can take him to court to correct the problem. However, in international trade, one can resort to the courts in the other party's country, but this is a long and tedious, if not impossible, solution. No, you must have full confidence in the other party in order to have any real success in international trade.

International trade is hardly new. There are numerous examples that show man has traded with people in other lands since pre-historic times. The spur to early trade was to obtain goods not available in your own area. Indeed, this is still the reason for much of today's world trade, e.g. petroleum and coffee.

With the growth of means of transportation it became practical to send goods from any source to almost anywhere. In the 19th Century a concept named "comparative advantage" became the base for determining the optimum level of total world production. The reasoning here was that, while a nation may have a comparative advantage in producing and exporting a good, i.e. it costs less to produce the product in the country, it may be more productive for it to concentrate on producing items in which it enjoys a better comparative advantage and leave others, where it also has a comparative advantage, to others who may not have the same level of comparative advantage, but allows them to produce and export goods that provide them with the funds to import. The full concept was to build a world trade that maximized total production by all nations.

This concept became the underlying basis for the complex pattern of production and trade around the world which we have come to call the "Global Economy." Again, the operative idea here is that one must allow all nations to engage in production so that they all have the means to import from others.

Another aspect of this developed concept of "comparative advantage" is that it allows us to rationalize the world's labor force to fully employ all work forces, thus yielding maximum production for all nations.

Of course, marshalling the world to achieve this maximum utilization of all work forces is difficult to achieve. However, it is the concept behind the theory of free trade which postulates allowing goods to move freely in world trade, unhindered by tariffs or bans on imports. If we have free trade throughout the world, then comparative advantage should be able to work in such a way as to maximize the world's total production.

Needless to add, while the theories are well packaged and taught in all economics curricula, implementing them is complex beyond our present capacities to fully accomplish. Over the last two centuries we have seen an acceleration of bringing about rationalization of the world's work forces and maximizing production, however, we have not totally mastered the system.

While we have not fully implemented comparative advantage and its mechanism for working, free trade, we enjoy more total world production today via free trade and adherence to comparative advantage than ever before. And we can expect this favorable trend to continue.

MOTIVATION VS STRUCTURE

While comparative advantage is the basic concept for the structure of world trade, we must also look at the demand for trade. In my book the main motivation for world trade today is our more consumer-oriented economies. The basic force for trade today is the simple concept that the consumer demands the best product possible at the best price possible. Note, I do not say cheapest price, but best price. You can make a good cheaper by reducing its quality or ability to supply the consumers expectations, e.g. Cadillac vs Chevrolet. The trick is to get the value to price right.

The eternal hunt for the best possible product at the best possible price is the main stimulus for world trade today. The search is made more acute given the huge steps we have made in facilitating transportation of goods from all points of the globe to all points of the globe. The other shot in the arm for this hunt is the internet and other means of communication. One can find the product he seeks literally anywhere in the world.

FOREIGN INVESMENT

It is impossible to divorce global trade from foreign investment, which means investment from sources in one country, into another country. There is a pattern that one sees in exporting from one country to another. You first enter with your products through an agent in the other country, usually an importer who specializes in bringing goods from other lands. However, when sales reach a certain level, you move to establishing your own import platform in the foreign destination, call it a business investment. The next step is, when sales merit the move, to build your own production facility in the foreign land, a capital investment.

The business and capital investments are what are generally referred to as "foreign investments." Not all exports merit these investments and are adequately handled by foreign agents. Much of my own work in the private and public sectors was devoted to deciding or helping others decide which formula worked best for their level of sales. I guided others in making these decisions, built business investments and capital investments, and even managed some of these structures.

There is another take on foreign investment. Some producers have established business or capital investments in other lands to buy or make products to send back to their own country. While the world generally sees these investments as using money created in one's home country to create jobs in another land, with the implied loss of jobs in one's homeland, they are a fact of life.

THE GLOBAL ECONOMY

So, in a nutshell this is the foreign trade and investment
that make up the "global economy." l use quotation marks
because, as I stated in my introduction, this international
movement of goods and services does not take into account
all the other elements of the actual global economy, e.g.
government income and expenditure, production for one's
own market, domestic investment in infrastructure,
domestic expenditure for health care, and more. We are
talking here about the relationships between the economies
of different countries, not the economy of each country
itself or all the economies of the world combined.

My work over more than 50 years has been to build these
relationships between nations, first as an American
diplomat and second as a private businessman. In doing so
I have collected a very diverse and descriptive set of tales,
often whimsical, that listeners always find entertaining and
instructive. By reading these, one can gain a better insight
into how the global economy actually works in practice and
how it affects various people. Thus, this book.

LEARNING THE TRADE

From a tender age I had a fascination with the world. At age ten I could name all the nations in Europe and their capitals when most others my age were still trying to remember all the US states and their capitals. I grew up in Washington DC so was exposed to the many foreign missions in the town and other links to the world around us. I set my sights on learning about the world and seeing as much of it as I could.

In college I decided on seeing the world through economic eyes. I saw that the future of our foreign relations would be for politics to give way to economics as the dominant concern. And the global economy has given me the way to see the world and learn about it.

To reach my goal of seeing the world via the global economy I focused my college studies on economics and my first love geography. I became very familiar with trade patterns between the many lands, many of which go back hundreds of years. My studies were made real by my work, while still in college, for the US Department of Agriculture in my hometown, Washington DC. I called this my "government scholarship" since it paid for my last two years of college. My official title was student-trainee and in order to keep my "scholarship" I had to include agricultural economics in my studies. Fortunately, agricultural economics was then considered to be the most developed and refined field in economic studies. Thus, I had excellent actual experience to supplement my formal studies.

Through my work with the department I gained a full insight into US agriculture. My actual work was to take data from our census reports and through linear regression fill in the years between when the censuses were actually taken, i.e. ten years apart. I was also charged with fitting curves to the data, using the same regression analysis, to show trends. My work was part of the elaborate model that matched farm sales to expenditures and through this come up with average net incomes. Contrary to popular belief, government subsidies to farmers are based, not on losses caused by price falls, but on average incomes, compared to a standard model calculated to provide a minimum standard of living for farmers. In other words, the subsidies were calculated to bring a farmer's income up to a minimum standard of living.

I did include agricultural economics in my studies. I recall a particularly interesting and useful course, International Agricultural Agreements. Hardly any agricultural item in international trade does not come under an international agreement, coffee, cocoa, and wheat to name the largest in

volume. My studies in this course gave me a first-hand
look at how products move in international trade.

PEACE CORPS

With this basic understanding I left college for the world.
My first destination was Ethiopia where I went as a member
of the first Peace Corps group sent to that country. In fact,
we were the first large contingent of Peace Corps
Volunteers to go anywhere, so early in the game, we had
our going away party in the White House with President
John Kennedy.

I was assigned to teach geography at the top high school in
Asmara, then the provincial capital of Eritrea and now the
capital of an independent Eritrea. While not engaged in the
global economy directly, I did teach geography to those
who would be the country's leaders. I say this since our
students were literally the cream of the crop of youngsters
in the country. There were only some 600 high school
teachers, half of those Peace Corps Volunteers, in the entire
country of 25 million. You can get an idea of how hard it
was to gain a place in a school.

In a curious quirk I also became the coach of the school's
football or soccer team. Imagine the consternation caused

by an American showing Ethiopians how to play their game. I faced considerable opposition that all faded away when I took the team to their first league championship in memorable history. You see, while my school had the smartest youngsters, it was traditionally lacking in athletic prowess. I had played the game as a kid but certainly did not have the ball handling skills of my players. However, I had played American football in high school and college so understood the basics of putting a team together and preparing them for competition.

By my second year as coach no one questioned my abilities or methods. I recall reading a newspaper report on the coming season for the high school league. The news article underlined the fact that the high school league was considered to be the highest level of all sports competition in Asmara, a city then of over 200,000. Sort of like a small town in West Texas where high school football is the talk of the town.

All talk of sport revolved around the league and thus there was considerable speculation about me. The article reviewed the players and coaches of each school giving most attention to our archrivals, who were coached by a player from Ethiopia's National Team. Our archrivals were tipped to win the championship, but the article ended by saying, "But then Haile Selassie High has Cecchini as its coach." There it was, no matter who was playing and coaching where, I was the magician coaching my school's team. I delivered, we won the school championship for the second year in a row, a feat that had never happened before nor since. I became a legend and am told that I am still known in the city as "The Coach."

Ten years after I left Asmara I was back for a visit. In my first stop in Addis Ababa, Ethiopia's capital I found some of my old players, two of them working for the national bank of Ethiopia, one had become Ethiopia's first home grown gynecologist, and others in various government ministries. In Asmara my main guide was a former player who worked for the city's chamber of commerce. Surprisingly I found another former player in the nation's largest seaport, Missawa, managing the best hotel in the city.

My Peace Corps work did yield a group of young men engaged in various pursuits relevant to the Global Economy.

FOREIGN SERVICE.

From the Peace Corps I entered the Foreign Service at the Department of State. I took the exams as a candidate for

the economics cone, a new specialty at State, recognizing
the increasing importance of economic relations in foreign
affairs. I chose this field because in university I became
convinced that economics, rather than politics, would be the
dominant factor in our foreign relations in the future. I was
proven correct when the "Global Economy" took center
stage in our foreign relations by the end of the 20th Century.
State gave me the opportunity to work directly in the global
economy and accumulate a wide range of experiences in
business, as well as important contacts.

NOW TO WORK

THE PANAMA PAPERS

Nothing like the topic of money laundering and hiding funds to start one off in his diplomatic career. Panama was my first diplomatic post. And when one hears this name he immediately thinks of the so-called "Panama Papers" of recent history that reported people from all over the world hiding money in Panama.

In Panama I was charged with finding hidden money. I was instructed to search the records of the BANCO PANAMANEO-SUIZO (Panamanian – Swiss Bank) to find accounts held there by the Fifth Avenue Coach Company in New York City. Most old timers will remember this iconic company that ran double decker buses up and down Fifth Avenue in the city. Well it seems that at one point the company was acquired by the Mafia which turned it into a company owning, not buses, but coin operated machines. This was, and is, a favorite way to launder funds gained from illegal activities. The Feds got word that the company held some of these ill-gotten gains in the Banco Panameno-Suizo and at the time the bank had been seized by Panamanian authorities, who believed it was insolvent.

I got permission to search the bank's records to see what funds the company held there. In those days we got whatever we asked for from the Panamanians. What a tedious job. I had to read the official records which were done in nearly impossible to read handwritten entries in Spanish. I soldiered on and went through the heavy tomes of the bank.

After this seemingly interminable task I came to two conclusions, first, the Fifth Avenue Coach Company did not have any accounts in the bank, and second, based on the official accounts, the bank was solvent and should not go through bankruptcy. Proof of my second conclusion came when the Panamanian authorities reopened the bank and invited all depositors to come claim their funds. If the bank had been insolvent the authorities would not have been able to reimburse all the depositors, but it did.

Of course, the answer to my findings being contrary to the original conclusion of the authorities that the bank was insolvent, and the missing accounts of the Fifth Avenue Coach Company, was that there were many accounts held "off the books." In other words, the official records did not report these accounts. So, it was no surprise to me to see the "Panama Papers" reveal these secret accounts, it was simply the long-time practice of holding accounts off the official records.

Imagine my surprise a year later, while in Washington, to find the end of the story. A magazine article reported that a body had been found floating in Lake Zurich with a bullet hole between its eyes. The article went to say that the body was that of the former director of the defunct Banco Panameno-Suizo. The hot money boys got revenge for their lost accounts.

ARMS SMUGGLING

Perhaps an even more sexy topic in world trade and finance is arms smuggling, taking arms to countries or areas where they are banned by international or national law. This is a wild and wooly field filled with eccentric, enigmatic, and yes, colorful, desperados, carefully working through the mine fields of mercenary armies, despots, rebels, freedom fighters, drug dealers, terrorists, megalomaniacs, and law enforcement around the world to make very lucrative sales. I know what these "merchants of death" are like, I met and dealt with one of the most famous at the time.

We got a cable at our embassy in Panama instructing us to have the local government seize and hold a World War II bomber flying into Panama that very day. We called the airport and told them to seize and hold the plane. Again, in those days the Panamanians did whatever we asked.

The crew of the plane immediately came to the embassy to protest the seizure. We told the crew that we had been instructed by Washington to seize the plane with no explanation given. They were not happy and worse, they were a very tough looking group that looked to be drawn out of the old "Terry and The Pirates" comic strips, you know, a hard-nosed captain leading the flotsam and jetsam of the South China Sea in questionable exploits. We were relieved when they left in a huff.

Later that day we got a call from the crew's hotel saying the crew had departed leaving an envelope for the embassy. I retrieved the envelope and, when we opened it at the embassy, found it contained the plane's papers and keys. Since it was my case, I became the unofficial owner of a World War II twin engine bomber. I took to taking my dates out to the airport to impress them with my airplane.

After a while I reminded my boss that we still had the plane and, while I was proud to be the "owner" of such an impressive aircraft, we really should resolve the matter. She told me to call Washington, which I did, and found that the matter was being handled, not by US Customs, but the office of munitions control. Thus, the plane was not, as we suspected, involved in drugs or some other illicit cargo, but was itself the object of the seizure. I was told that indeed the matter had been resolved and a Mr. Smith would be arriving soon to take the plane back to the USA.

Imagine my surprise when a few days later a Mr. Jones arrived at the embassy to claim the plane. I told him that I could not do this since I was to give it to Smith. Jones explained that Smith could not come, so he was there in his place. I told him I would have to have further instruction from Washington. He asked if we could to this by phone since he was pressed to get the plane back to the USA. I got permission and called the Office of Munitions Control. The office confirmed Jones' story and instructed me to turn over the plane to him. Thank God I followed good practice and took the name of the person and office at State that gave me the order.

I turned the papers and keys over to Jones and reminded him that he had to pay the storage charges at the airport to get its release. He rushed off to claim his plane.

I should add here that, while waiting to call Washington and for a response, Jones told me the story of the plane. He was taking it back to Florida to be outfitted as a flying camera platform to film a new movie being made at the time, "The Battle For Britain," which was actually made and became a box office success. He described in detail

what had to be done to the plane to allow it to do the job.
He also talked at length about how the film was to be made.

Thank goodness I had been prudent. A few hours after
giving Jones the keys I got a call from the Office of
Munitions Control. In a panic they said there had been an
error in instructing me to hand over the plane and could I
get the Panamanians to seize it again. I explained that,
while the Panamanians did whatever we asked, I did not
want to look like a fool and test their patience.   The office
asked if I could insure that Jones brought the plane back to
Florida. I asked if they wanted me to ride "shotgun" on the
plane? We decided on tracking the plane through the FAA
facility in the Panama Canal Zone.

Jones did not leave for several days but, when he did, I
went to the FAA facility and sat with the flight controllers
who tracked the plane back to Florida. Afterwards I finally
got a cable from Washington congratulating the embassy
for a job well done. It seems that several American war
planes had been taken from the USA and flown through
Central America and South America to Brazil from where
they were being flown, in violation of official bans, to the
war then raging in Biafra, Nigeria. We had successfully
prevented this from happening to this plane.

But the story didn't end then. A year later I was reading an article in a magazine in Washington about the black market for illegal weapons. The article talked about several items but noted that the most desired weapons in this trade were war planes. It went on to reveal that the most dangerous person in the illegal sale of controlled war planes was, you guessed it, my Mr. Jones. The article described him exactly as I remembered him. I suddenly realized that I had handed over my plane to the world's most notorious war plane smuggler. However, in my case, he took the plane back to Florida, where it was used in filming the movie.

NARCOTICS

No tale about a Latin American country would be complete without talking about the impact of the global drug trade. Panama was not immune. The business came home to me when I refused to issue a visa for a Panamanian diplomat, its consul in Genoa, Italy. Now this was not your run of the mill diplomat, he was in fact an Italian who had fled the country following WWII. You see, he had been on Mussolini's team. He found refuge in Panama by, I am sure, bribing the right authority or authorities. Not only did he find refuge in Panama, he managed to work his way into a prize consular post abroad, in his home country, where he could operate with the immunity granted by his diplomatic status.

I refused the visa because we had information that he had been seized in the Toronto airport with a briefcase filled with cocaine. The Canadians kept the drugs but let him go. I said I would not issue him a visa. The Panamanian Foreign Ministry responded with an official demarche or demand rejecting our refusal of the visa and demanding we issue one. I was alone, the rest of the embassy, including my boss and the ambassador, felt we should overlook the drug dealing report and simply give him a transit visa that would only cover his going through a US airport en route to Europe. I said, that is all he wants, the ability to drop off a briefcase in the US and continue on with the money paid. I lost the argument and the "narco" got his visa.

ATOMS FOR PEACE

Only the older members of our society will recall the effort in the 1950s and 1960s to promote peaceful uses of atomic energy in a calculated strategy to lessen fear of the new technology known throughout the world for nuclear weapons. We put on a very elaborate traveling show about peaceful uses of atomic energy which I handled. The exhibits included a proposed building with atomic bombs of a new sea level canal through Panama to connect the Pacific with the Caribbean. The sea level canal would avoid the elaborate lock system used to raise and lower boats through the old canal.

The sea level canal project was dropped when scientists began to calculate the residual dangers left by blasting a canal through Panama with atomic bombs. In fact, the only use of nuclear energy found then to be useful was the production of electric energy which became the new favorite way to meet our rapidly growing demand for electric power. This ushered in a wave of building nuclear power plants around the world until the arrival of President Jimmy Carter, but more about that later.

OTHER TALES FROM PANAMA

WAR AND PEACE

While the stories above were probably the most directly related to the global economy, I had other adventures in Panama. There was the one where I got directly involved in a pending war between two Indian tribes. I had visited the San Blas Islands off the Caribbean coast of Panama. There I met an American living on a catamaran docked near a village of the Cuna Indians. He was building a resort on one of the islands. A prime example of US foreign investment at the grass roots level.

Now the San Blas Islands are barely above sea level so there was limited economic opportunity other than some basic agriculture. The men were heavily recruited to work on the Panama Canal, which took them away from their families for long periods of time.

The San Blas Indian women left behind became famous for sewing their colorful applique blouses with elaborate designs that have earned them a worldwide reputation as works of art. Making the blouses was introduced to the island's ladies by Christian missionaries who were appalled by the Cuna practice of the women simply painting their naked breasts. To replace this immodest practice the missionaries showed the ladies how to turn the elaborate body paintings into colorful blouses that became the world famous "Molas" of the Cuna Indians.

There is no fresh water in the Cuna's San Blas islands, except for limited amounts collected from roofs during rain. Most fresh water comes from the mainland where the Cuna go on daily trips in dugout canoes to fetch water from small rivers. The Cuna had also adopted the practice of farming small plots of land where they would go for water.

The Cuna water sourcing and limited farming on the mainland would not be a problem except that the area from where they drew the water and farmed the land was the domain of the Choco Indians, a very reclusive group who lived in houses isolated from each other. The Choco felt the Cunas were "stealing their land." The Cuna responded with complaints that the Choco would steal their women when the men went off to work on the canal. War drums started to rumble.

My American contact called me urgently at the embassy to report the pending war between the two tribes. I went to the Foreign Ministry to report the danger. The Foreign Ministry thanked me for the report and the government took measures to prevent the war. I literally helped stop a war that would have seen bows and arrows against small arms.

BAD PRESS

Then there was the case where I appeared on the front page of a local newspaper accused of refusing to issue a visa to a leading journalist. The actual fact was that he was one of the few card-carrying members of the small Communist Party in Panama. US visa law prevents issuing visas to Communists and I had applied the law. So how, you might ask, did Communists get visas? In each case a waiver of

the law was requested, and I told the journalist this. He
preferred to make it an issue in the news.

We resolved the case by obtaining a waiver but that left my
image a bit tattered. Fortunately, our information section
took advantage of a young lad, about ten years old, going to
the USA on an exchange program. The next day the press
was filled with a photo showing me handing a visa to the
young man for his trip.

FANNY FOX

Many old timers will also remember the case of the
Argentine ecdysiast Fanny Fox. She and then Congressman
Wilber Mills were saved from a car that Mills had driven
into the Tidal Basin, a tributary of Washington's Potomac
River. By then I was back in Washington preparing to
marry my wife. I recall her reading from an article in the
news in which a reporter covering the Fox case started by
saying, "Natasha at the Silver Slipper," the club where Fox
was performing in DC, "told him that …." I cut her short
by saying, "I know Natasha and she will tell you whatever
you want to hear if you buy her a drink." Astounded she
asked me if I knew Natasha, I replied, "I know Fanny Fox."
You see, Fanny was performing in Panama when I was

there, and I was introduced to her at her club by a friend. I believe I subsequently issued her a visa to go to the USA.

BEYOND PANAMA

Panama was my introduction to actually being involved in the global economy and how it works   Rather than discuss these in a country by country account, I will talk about them under subject classes and refer to the country in which they occurred.

TRADE

TRADE GONE WRONG

Perhaps the most egregious case of trade deals gone wrong faced me in Turkey where I was our Commercial Attache during the country's experience with socialism under then Prime Minister Bulent Ecevit. The country was technically bankrupt and left with no foreign exchange to buy essential imports. To show how serious it was, Turkey could not afford to import coffee. Imagine that, Turkey without Turkish coffee.

The problem I faced was representing dozens of American companies who had not been paid for their exports to Turkey, a debt in the hundreds of millions of dollars. The companies wanted their money and refused to export any more goods to the country.

To keep the economy afloat the US, as well as several other wealthy countries, were extending long term loans to allow Turkey to import essential goods that most realized would never be repaid. Our specific program was one invented during the Vietnam War called balance of payments funding. In it we simply handed over millions of dollars for the Turks to use to pay for imports. I know, I actually handed over several such checks to the Turks. Nothing so empowering as to hand over a check for $5 million.

I argued that these funds should at least be used only to import American items so, while we may not ever be repaid, the funds would be used to buy American goods. I was overruled by my colleagues who insisted the funds be "untied" so the Turks could use them for whatever they wanted to import, most importantly petroleum. They countered my arguments with claims that all the donor countries extending these "soft" loans to the Turks were following this policy. I reported that the actual case was that the other countries were indeed "tying" their loans to buying products from their countries. My reports of the actual practice were rejected and we continued to play the sucker.

"BAD COP"

During my two stints at our embassy in Madrid, Spain I was charged with handling trade disputes with the Spanish. The US was constantly laying "countervailing duties" on our main imports from Spain. This was easily done since our rules in those times did not call for demonstration that Spanish imports were damaging our industries. One could request a countervailing duty without showing any harm being done or, in fact, one could request a countervailing to head off any potential import.

The most ridiculous case here was a US company requesting a countervailing duty against imports of vitamin K from Spain. In fact, Spain had never exported vitamin K to the USA. However, the countervailing duty request sparked the Spanish to look into such exports and begin exporting vitamin K to the USA. Talk about unintended consequences.

The target for the countervailing duties was Spain's rebate program for exports. It is common practice for nations to rebate taxes paid on a good that is exported, many are familiar with this practice from experience in asking for rebates of taxes when they buy a product abroad and bring it home to the USA. With the VAT tax it is fairly straight forward, one is rebated the VAT tax on the product. However, the Spanish did not have a VAT tax, but rather, a tax applied on each stage of production known as a "cascading" tax which was not specific to the product itself. To determine how much tax to rebate, the Spanish calculated average taxes paid for each product. The countervailing duty was based on their inability to state the exact tax paid by each product.

I was constantly vilified by the Spanish shoe industry for representing our countervailing duties imposed on their hot selling shoe exports to the USA. I worked to soften the blow of these taxes on the shoes. My rationale was that we were running one of our few trade surpluses in the world with Spain. There was no reason to alienate the Spaniards, who were buying more from us, than what we bought from them.

Perhaps even more insulting to the Spaniards was our imposition of what was euphemistically known as "voluntary restraints" on Spanish exports of steel to the USA. Believe it or not we got the Spaniards to impose limits on their steel exports to the USA to avoid upsetting US manufacturers. Of course, the only reason they agreed to these self-imposed limits was that we threatened to impose countervailing duties on the steel.

I had to negotiate these several agreements in an atmosphere of trying to limit the hurt caused by the agreements. I was successful in getting the agreements signed. More importantly, on a trip to Spain sometime after the steel dispute, I was invited to dinner by the association of steel manufacturers in Spain. They then told me that they really appreciated the way I worked one agreement. It seems I had arranged the "voluntary restraints" to fall heavily on the state-owned steel mills and leave the private steel makers relatively unscathed. I thanked them for their compliments, but kept to myself the fact that I really hadn't had that in mind when I worked out the deal.

Through these tariff agreements I became a recognized expert in the use of tariffs, how to implement them and how to enforce them.

THE GRANDDADDY OF ALL TRADE PACTS

The most difficult trade agreements are those covering equipment, materials, technology and financing for the export of nuclear power plants. In the early 1970s then President Jimmy Carter upset the whole world of energy supply when he moved to change our bilateral agreements covering the export of US nuclear plants. Of course, one does not export a completed plant, but we ship the materials, equipment, technology and financing under very precise agreements.

Carter had a real concern about safeguarding the rear end of the nuclear fission cycle. In an atomic nuclear power plant, the enriched uranium is burned in very complex power stations with complete controls over the use and handling of the enriched uranium. Carter's concern, however, was how the spent or burned fuel was handled, the so-called "back end" of the nuclear power cycle. I took to saying Jimmy Carter had spent too many years wearing lead underpants in nuclear submarines.

The model adopted by all the countries for handling the "back end" of the nuclear fuel cycle was to take the spent fuel and recycle it to produce three products, first, still usable enriched fuel to send back to the reactor at the center of the power station, second, plutonium to use in the next generation of nuclear power plants called "breeder" reactors, and finally real waste material. Perfect solution since the unused enriched fuel would be recovered and used, we would produce plutonium for our new breeder reactors and the actual waste would be reduced enormously, a pile of waste the size of a living room would be reduced to half a wine bottle of waste.

Breeder reactors were even more promising than nuclear reactors. The breeder reactor actually produces more fuel while consuming the plutonium, a process I admit I never did fully understand. Our energy future was assured, we would have an almost endless supply of electric energy.

But Carter was too concerned with plutonium to allow this dream solution to our energy problems go forward. At the time the news was filled with tales of the so-called "basement" bombs which were explosive devices girded with plutonium. The bombs would not ignite the plutonium to produce a hydrogen bomb, it takes an atomic bomb to ignite a hydrogen bomb, but it would spew plutonium over the countryside and one speck of plutonium is enough to kill a person.

To prevent this from happening Carter took specific steps which he called "full scope safeguards." First, he canned our breeder reactor program (the French and Japanese refused to follow suit). Second, he demanded that we have new agreements with our clients to cover continued export of US nuclear power plants.

At the time American companies were building some eight new nuclear power plants in Spain, the largest exposure for our Export-Import Bank loans for one type of sale, in one country, ever. We are talking maybe $8 billion in 1970 dollars.

As the energy officer at the time at our embassy I got the instructions from Washington to renegotiate our nuclear agreements with Spain. I told my boss that this was going to be a long, hard slog. After reviewing the instructions, I told him we should sign four new agreements to replace the one in place. The first three would be rather straight forward and readily adopted. However, the fourth was near impossible.

The fourth agreement covered how the spent fuel from the nuclear power stations would be handled. Under our in-place agreement it was to be sent to the UK for reprocessing in the future to get plutonium for the new breeder reactors. I said, if the issue was to have complete control over the spent fuel, it was much better to send it to the UK, where it would be under tight security, rather than make it stay in Spain, which was totally unprepared to handle spent fuel. My arguments failed, Carter insisted that all spent fuel must remain in the country where it was produced.

I knew this would be hard because it would commit the Spaniards to untold expense in creating storage for spent fuel in Spain. The country would reply that we had an agreement and the US must comply with it. And, indeed, that is what happened.

I then spent several months working with US agencies and the Spanish government to come up with a solution. I actually took all the positions from all sides and all demands and came up with an agreement that I wrote. I knew it was a winner, since I wrote it and didn't understand it. I was certain no one else would ever understand what it meant. It was signed by both sides. The only reason it was accepted was that it was an interim agreement to cover the next six months while we hammered out a permanent agreement. To prove how opaque the document was and impossible to decipher, the six-month agreement stood for nine years when it was replaced by our agreement with Euroatom on Spain entering the European Union in 1986. Talk about kick the can down the road.

 I had done the impossible, got the Spaniards to sign a new agreement that complied with President Carter's new rules. I had also saved the Eximbank's largest single exposure of credit ever, construction of eight new nuclear power stations in Spain. My reward was to be reassigned to Washington to assist in the effort to get all our other nuclear cooperation agreements renegotiated. Afterall, I was the only person who had managed to construct an acceptable agreement.

Unfortunately, I found that the apparatus created to do the renegotiating job was way off the mark and doomed to failure. I opted to go back abroad. To prove the wisdom of my calculation the program broke up on what could be called a touch of poetic justice. The first country to agree to signing a new agreement with the USA that contained "full scope safeguards" was Iran. This critical first step was destroyed when the Shah was overthrown and our embassy seized, with its staff held as prisoners for over one year. Carter's bold new plan crashed on the rocks in Iran, supreme irony since the seizure of our embassy was the main reason he lost reelection. I call it poetic justice.

AIRCRAFT

One of the most widely traded items in world trade are aircraft. This is a very competitive field dominated by a few very large enterprises. A truly major test for any sales team.

One of the first calls I made on arrival at our embassy in Helsinki, Finland was to see the president of its flagship airline, FinnAir. We congratulated each other on the new air route we had established, direct flights from Helsinki to California via Seattle flying over the vast Arctic near the North Pole.

I asked the FinnAir president, who was perhaps more important than the president of the nation, since his company was a major engine for the Finnish economy, what else could I do for him. He immediately replied, "We want to buy two of your aircraft." The actual buy was to purchase two giant DC 10 aircraft from McDonnell Douglas Aircraft that were being built for Egypt Air which cancelled the purchase following a major tragedy involving a new DC 10. A DC 10 crashed after takeoff from Chicago's O'Hare airport killing all 271 on board the year before. That crash, after an even more fatal one a few years earlier when a DC 10 crashed after takeoff in Paris in which 346 died, led to the plane being called a "death trap." In spite of its bad reputation, the president of Finnair told me that the plane was a good one and his pilots liked it.

The key ingredient of the sale, however, was that the president said FinnAir would insist on the same financing that we had extended to Egypt Air. I said no problem and went back to the embassy to report what was a major export opportunity for the USA. I got kudos for the proposal but with a deal killing caveat, we could not extend the same financing terms we had given Egypt Air to FinnAir. The rationale was that while Egypt Air represented a "poor" country that we wanted to assist with very favorable financing via our Eximbank, FinnAir was a wealthy carrier in a wealthy country.

Now I knew our Eximbank from my work for them in Spain where I saved their bacon on what was at the time its largest extension of credit in history for the export of eight nuclear power stations, which I have reported elsewhere in this book. The Eximbank is a US Government operation that has provided financing for major exports until recently when it has been undergoing a reorganization and reevaluation. Aircraft are its bread and butter and practically no export of major commercial aircraft takes place without its financing.

Exim was convinced the Finns had to buy the aircraft so would get our normal finance terms. I replied that they were wrong, I explained that I knew the Finns were playing on the bad reputation of the plane, which gave them a strong hand in the deal. I noted that the Finns knew that it was a propitious time for the move and they were buying the planes well in advance of its long term plans in order to get the very generous financing offered to Egypt Air. Even more to the point, I noted, that after the crash the year before, we should be happy to find any buyer for the planes and that the sale to FinnAir would help restore the aircraft's reputation.

I had let our ambassador know about the opportunity and he took an active interest in what would be a major US export to Finland. I told him about Exim's deal killing reply and that we had to be directly involved in the transaction to make it work. A career officer, he was reluctant to get into a battle with Washington. I asked him to let me handle it since I knew Exim and how it operated, a bold move for any person in my position.

After discussing the deal with McDonnel Douglas's main man for the sale I returned to the ambassador and asked him to offer a dinner for the McDonnell Douglas team that was to visit Finland to pursue the deal. He agreed and held a dinner for the company's head man and his agent for the sale. I led the discussion which was, in essence, a learning exercise for the ambassador who, while he held a technical background from having negotiated many of our nuclear agreements, was new to how to make a major sale work. At one point I boldly asked our visitors if they had paid the loan commitment fee to Exim which was essentially an earnest payment to secure financing. They replied no and I went way out beyond normal practice by instructing them to pay the fee. If I proved to be wrong, I, and the ambassador, would have received major complaints that would have been a black mark on my record.

McDonnell paid the loan commitment fee. I bolstered this move by sending in a stream of reports about the sale emphasizing the key role financing would play. I continued to reject Exim's insistence on normal financing.

I came home one evening to see on the evening news a DC 10 taking off. I did not speak Finnish but realized that this meant the Finns had bought the planes. The next morning I was greeted by the ambassador who had had a most interesting experience the day before. He had been called from Washington to say that we had sold the planes to Finland. However, when he asked with what financing terms, he was told the normal terms, which by then he knew were not acceptable. His confusion was allayed when he subsequently received a call from the president of FinnAir to congratulate him on the sale. The ambassador responded how was that possible when the terms were not the favorable ones, but our normal terms. The president laughed, "Oh that was what Exim's staff had offered, but they were overruled by the president of bank who instructed them to do the sale with the special EgyptAir terms."

The ambassador was elated, he had never seen how an embassy could make a difference in a major export deal. I simply replied, "It must have been those convincing cables you sent Washington." You see, all cables from an embassy are signed off by the ambassador, no matter who actually writes them. I had done all of the ones related to this sale and thus gained a big gold star from the ambassador. I was also relieved that my game plan had worked.

In a very fine gesture from Finnair, the ambassador and I were invited with our wives to go on Finnair's inaugural flight on its new route from Helsinki to Seattle and Los Angeles. The offer met with resistance from others at the embassy since they believed it could be seen as an unacceptable gift. I had to secure Washington's approval for the flight. I sent off a couple of messages focusing on the amazing opportunity the flight would give the ambassador and me to share a major event with key Finnish government and business contacts and thereby improve our relations with them. Washington replied, "Cogent argument from embassy convinces us to approve your participation in the flight."

I had a small problem. My wife had just given birth to our second child in Finland who was only few months old. She did not want to leave her with others at such a tender age so I asked Finnair if we could take her with us. The airline agreed and our newborn daughter was the youngest passenger on FinnAir's historic first direct flight over the North Pole to California. The flight must have had some impact on her since these many years later she has made San Francisco her home.

Nothing like brokering a major sale of some $200 million worth of airplanes to prove your export smarts.

TRADE SHOWS

Not all of my trade promotion efforts were successful. One of the most visible aspects of international trade are "trade shows" in which sellers bring their newest items to the market to gain attention. These shows are held everywhere and for all goods and services. My youngest daughter is an animator, as is her husband. They make a practice to attend trade shows when they can in order to keep up with what is happening in that fascinating field.

Official US Government sponsored exhibits in trade shows are a staple for all US commercial offices around the world. I thought we had missed a major opportunity to show our stuff. In the 1970's few of my colleagues at our embassy in Madrid would venture to the Basque area in northern Spain. We had a consulate in the largest city there, Bilbao. The reason few dared go there was it was the height of the Basque separatists' lethal campaign to break away from Spain. All businesses were forced to pay protection money to the clandestine rebels and those who refused suffered either damage to their enterprises or harm to their owners, with assassinations common.

Undaunted I went there on business trips to maintain contact with the many firms engaged in foreign trade. I was impressed by the Basques. Not many knew that in the 1970s the Basque areas enjoyed the highest average incomes in Spain, the best education levels, the best health care, and more. But all this good did not outweigh the primal need for "freedom," which in Basque terms meant independence from Spain and a place for their unique culture and language to flourish. The rebels were steadily destroying a remarkably successful economy in pursuit of independence.

In my work to maintain our commercial presence in this vital area I learned that the USA had never had a presence in what was Spain's premier industrial trade show, The Feria De Muestras de Bilbao, The Bilbao Products Fair. With a great deal of argument I finally convinced Washington to put up a US exhibit at the show. The team who constructed the show were very good with the head a true veteran of our trade shows. They constructed a very attractive exhibit with a good group of US companies on full display.

Imagine my elation the day the fair opened and I arrived for the opening ceremonies. Imagine my distress when it became apparent that few visitors were coming to the show. All dressed up for the ball and no music. The first day was a total disaster with a paucity of visitors. The only saving grace was that, most who did come, were actual businessmen looking for new products, the intent of the fair. This fair was traditionally the biggest commercial event of the year in Bilbao with thousands of business visitors and the general public. The second and third days were no better. A real fiasco.

What happened? Well after the fair I found that the Basque armed separatists had threatened to bomb the show. While never reported because the government wanted to keep it quiet, word got around and the crowds kept away in fear of being a victim. My error, in my passion to create a US commercial presence in Bilbao, I had overlooked the separatist threat.

I believe I am still used at the Department of Commerce as the example of how not to do a trade show.

TRADE IN SERVICES

Everyone is familiar with trade in products, but most have no clue about trade in services. The US has traditionally held trade surpluses in service trade while continuing to incur tremendous deficits in goods trade. However, our government in general is unable to comprehend or promote service exports.

TOURISM

Believe it or not the US earns more money from foreign visitors than any other country. However, we also spend more than any other country, so we usually run a deficit on foreign tourism.

On my second assignment to Spain, this time as our Commercial Attache, I developed a plan to promote trade in services. I selected as the markets to be addressed tourism, financial services and entertainment. No other embassy had developed such a plan and we had to lead Washington in this venture.

Tourism in Spain is like talking about coffee in Brazil. It is the epitome of a country that has used tourism to move into the ranks of the worlds' prosperous nations. It holds a massive tourism sector trade fair every other year called FITUR. The fair staff had been repeatedly turned down by our embassy when approached to be an exhibitor.

I said no, it was time to show our stuff in this premier tourism trade show.

I got permission from Washington to participate with one small condition, Washington could not give us any funds to do the show. I accepted the challenge.

As a vehicle to conduct our participation I created the "Visit USA
Committee" which included representatives of US companies working in Spain. At our first meeting I told the committee that I would not be a part of the committee and would hold no funds collected for the effort. I would be an "adviser" to the committee. The reason for this was to avoid Washington coming in and taking over the work and more importantly, having to send the funds raised to Washington and asking for it back. You see, Washington insisted in having all funds used for a promotion being held in Washington and not at post. This was no minor rule, I temporarily replaced a colleague at our Trade Center in

Milan, Italy who had been fired for mishandling promotion funds.

We asked the fair authorities for a good space in their main building, after all, we were the USA. They replied with some bad locations in the main hall which I rejected. They then offered us an entire building between two exhibit halls. I agreed but then faced the challenge of filling a huge building with an unknown number of exhibitors.

In the actual case the committee, which is still housed in the commercial section of our embassy in Madrid, did a fantastic job of recruiting US exhibitors and we had something like 50 companies join us for the fair. Even with 50 we had lots of excess space which we filled with a massive stage on which we presented American entertainment using local American talent (you would be amazed at how many American performers make foreign cities their homes).

I realized that the committee needed at least one full time staff and introduced them to the spouse of an embassy employee who had substantial experience in tourism, who they contracted to do the job. I made sure she handled all the funds and took all instructions from the committee and not me.

In another smart move I made an agreement with a small private university in Madrid, that specialized in giving sound education in business, to use its advanced students in our exhibition. In exchange for this valuable hands-on experience in private business, the students provided all the staff we needed to man the 50 exhibits, along with company representatives coming from the USA, at no charge.   The agreement was subsequently copied by several other US government commercial offices in other embassies. I also became

a close friend of the school and was even invited to give a commencement address for one graduating class.

The show was a complete success. The head of the US Office for Tourism in our Department of Commerce came out to open the exhibit. She was totally impressed by what we had accomplished with no support from Washington. In spite of the accolades, I was subsequently grilled about my handling of the finances for the event. I was able to quash all accusations of improprieties by carefully noting that all finances were handled by the committee and its contracted staff. Once again, I outsmarted Washington.

In recognition of the important new asset the school got from its agreement with the embassy, after all, what other school could offer its students real experience in trade, I was asked to give the commencement address at the school's graduation ceremony. The commencement address was a bit comic. My wife and I were invited to the dinner for the graduating seniors at the school. As I sat there listening to the president of the school preview the evening's events, I was shocked to hear him say, "We are pleased to have as our keynote speaker a representative of the American Embassy." Of course, he meant me, and I had not prepared a speech. I spent the next hour or so furiously scribbling a speech on some napkins. In spite of its impromptu origins the speech was well received by the graduates.

Afterwards my good friend, who taught at the school, told me that he had never seen his students take such copious notes during their classes as they did during my speech.

I can assure you no other US Commercial Office could have pulled this one off, a whole new direction for our trade promotion program.

FINANCIAL SERVICES

BANKS

One of America's most lucrative exports are financial services. Our banks, insurance companies, financial services companies – read stockbrokers, and other money handlers - are the models for most other such institutions. Yes, London is a leading financial services center and so too are Switzerland and Hong Kong, but US firms in this field usually hold the high ground.

The difference here from other exports is that the service exporter has to usually be physically present in the market. And other countries make it very hard for them to operate.

My first experience in opening a new market for our financial services exports was in Finland. The Finns had by all accounts unwittingly opened the door to foreign banks when it changed its banking rules. At the time I was there as the head of our economics section at the embassy. I was introduced to an Englishman who had been hired by Citibank to open a branch in Finland. This was to be the first American bank to operate in the country. He told me that the Finns had been blocking him at every turn and asked for the embassy's help. I discussed the matter with our ambassador and got him to agree for me to intervene.

The Englishman said the Finns wanted him to get the embassy to send a letter to the Finnish government urging it to admit Citibank under the principle of reciprocity, since Finnish banks were already operating in the USA. I told the ambassador that he should not send such a letter, since it would have to be vetted in Washington until the cows came home.

I started by finding the poor sot in Finland's Finance Ministry who had been given the job of stalling the US bank's request to operate there. He admitted that the government had made a mistake in opening to foreign banks and he was charged with correcting the error. I told him that this was foolish, the new law was clear and, sooner or later, foreign banks would be coming into Finland. I worked with him to find ways to explain to his superiors why they had to loosen up and allow in foreign banks. We finally built him a way to allow the banks in and for him to keep his job.

With my work with the Finance Ministry man in hand I then went to the ambassador with a letter for him to send to the Finnish Government. In it I called for the Finns to accept US banks "in the spirit of reciprocity." He responded by reminding me that I had advised him against such a letter. I then told him that no one could be hanged for saying, "in the spirit of reciprocity," instead of demanding reciprocity. I told him I had already greased the rails with my Finance Ministry counterpart so all that was lacking was an official push from him.

The ambassador sent the letter and in a matter of days Citibank opened its doors in Helsinki. I must say, however, that the bank's man in Finland was not very generous in acknowledging my service to him and his bank. But the deed was done and other US banks quickly followed Bank of America's lead.

I literally opened the door for American banking into Finland.

INSURANCE

Perhaps an even more lucrative service export than banking for American companies is insurance. While the insurance business, as we know it, started with insuring ships and their cargoes by companies in London, England, and Lloyds of London is still the grand dame of the trade, American firms play a major role in this vital component of the global economy. As with our banks, our companies are the most formidable competitors in the field. As such, most other countries do what they can to keep us out of their markets or at least make it very difficult to enter.

I had another Englishman visit me, this time at my office in our embassy in Madrid, Spain where I was the Commercial Attache (never could understand the reason for American firms hiring Englishmen to manage their operations abroad.) He explained that his American employer, a large insurance firm named Alexander and Alexander, had bought a Spanish insurance firm through which to do business in Spain. However, when he went to take the new acquisition's seat in the "Colegio de Assegadoras," the "College of Insurers," he was told it could not occupy the seat and effectively could not do business. The reason he could not take the seat was that he was a foreign company and he had to prove that Spanish firms could do insurance business in the USA, before he could take the seat in the college. When he asked how to do this, he was told that he had to get a letter from the American Embassy stating that Spanish firms could do insurance business in the USA. Thus, his visit to the embassy.

I told my visitor that I could help him but on condition that he said nothing about what I was doing to anyone else in the embassy. I explained that if anyone else knew, I would have to go through a long, laborious process to get Washington's approval for my help and, in the actual case, I would probably not get the approval, since no one in Washington would really know what to do.

He accepted my condition and I immediately went to my typewriter and banged out a draft letter which I had reason to believe would do the job. I was inventing, since there was no established procedure for what I was doing. I handed the draft to my visitor who immediately asked if his legal person could review it. I said he could let anyone look at it outside the embassy, but once more said, do not show it to anyone in this building.

A few weeks later I remembered my visitor and called him to see what had happened. He asked if he could come in for a visit and did so the next day. He told me he had had his local legal person review the letter which they in turn sent to their regional headquarters in London. From there the letter went back to the head office of the company in Annapolis, Maryland. He then showed me my draft with corrections, additions and modifications made by the head office. In fact, there was only one addition, which I was pleased to see, because it showed that they understood what I was doing.

I told my visitor that if he agreed with the amended letter I would have it typed out by my secretary and sign it then and there. He enthusiastically said yes. I signed the letter with embassy letterhead and asked if he wanted me to send it to the college or did he want to take it himself. He opted to hand deliver it.

Shortly thereafter I got a call from the insurance man who exclaimed, "We are in!" He later came by my office to thank and take me out to lunch at the top sea food restaurant in a city that cherishes sea food.

So how did I do it, you might ask? The problem with making a statement that Spanish companies could do the same thing in the USA that my visitor's company could do in Spain is that our insurance industry is ruled by state, not federal law. There was no practicable way to get the assurance of all 50 state regulators that Spanish firms could do this.

My trick was to state in the letter I wrote that, "There was no US law that prevented Spanish insurance firms from doing business in the USA." Indeed, there are no federal laws stating who may do insurance business in the USA but there are 50 bodies of state law regulating this. The addition made by the company's head office recognized what I was doing by stating, "and there is no law in the State of Maryland preventing Spanish firms from doing business in the state." The Spanish authorities did not capture this fine distinction and approved the company taking the seat they had bought in the college.

This initial entry by an American firm into the insurance business in Spain opened a flood of followers and in rapid order American firms had developed billions of dollars worth of business in the Spanish insurance market.

Again, I had done the impossible, brought a whole new American industry to Spain.

WALL STREET

I found myself in New York City at the height of the dot.com bubble in the 1990s. My wife had taken the post as head of the State Department's Office of Foreign Missions there. She was the interface between the hundreds of consulates and missions to the UN and the city government. Since Rudi Giuliani was the mayor it was helpful for her to have an Italian surname.

But what was I to do? I was still closing down the South African Trade Center that I had built in Orlando, Florida. It was a prime example of what happens when you throw a party and no one comes. The South African investor who created the center wanted a place where South African exporters to the USA, following the lifting of sanctions after the election of Nelson Mandela as the first black president of the nation, could use as an entry point into the US market. The center had offices, a large show room and a warehouse for the exporters' operations. More on that under investments.

I looked around and found another new investment product that was selling like hot cakes, currency exchange. Some clever finance people in Hong Kong had hit on a way for the average investor to engage in currency trading, a major break-through since currency trades are a minimum $500,000 trade usually done between banks.

I found a company in what is "Little Korea," the cluster of buildings in the shadow of the Empire State Building owned by Koreans, that offered a platform for currency traders. I attended their introduction course where I met Dan Constantini, a real New Yorker. We were sitting in a presentation on various numbers theories used in currency trading. You see the real traders did not pay attention to world events, trade patterns, interest rate differentials between countries, economic expectations and natural disasters as do the average currency traders. No, they focus on number movements, or as I like to call it, "follow the bouncing ball." They stay in dark rooms illuminated by screens with currency movements. They then apply various number theories to the movements and make their calls based on this.

When the presenter mentioned the Fibonacci Series, Dan and I immediately replied by saying that this is one system for playing blackjack. We both realized that we were engaging in a game but, what we did not know, was that the game was rigged. Dan became a lifelong friend who is now playing in that "Great Casino in the Sky."

I learned that the Korean company was a scam, when I came back from a last trip to Orlando for the trade center, to find the entire building where I was learning to trade currencies cordoned off by that well-known police yellow tape barring entry. The management of the firm had been arrested and all properties, personal and company, were seized. Fortunately, I had nothing in the building but a few pads of paper and some pens.

I subsequently learned that most of the operations offering currency trading opportunities were bogus. The offer was to allow one to buy a share of a currency trade but the reality was that the companies were simply trading one investor's buy for another investor's sell and the whole business took place within the company's walls, a total fraud.

I took a friend's advice and fled to a stockbroker, Dean Whitter, where I took a test in a room full of would be Wall Street Whizzes, maybe 80 or so. I was one of the few, maybe five, selected for an interview. The interviewers were up front with me, they seldom hired people my age, 56, but my test scores were too impressive to overlook.

I should digress here a bit. All of my job offers when I graduated from the University of Maryland came from my test scores, not from my college work or other factors. I do very well on entrance exams and such. No surprise here, I am a member of Mensa.

The test that impressed me the most was when, as a graduating senior, I went to Baltimore to take the exam for entering the Federal Reserve System. There I was, the only candidate in a room with some 30-40 would-be-bankers, without a degree in accounting. Yes, I had studied statistics and worked my last two years in college as a statistician for the Department of Agriculture, my first paid job was as a bookkeeper at age 12 for my parents' bowling league, was the treasurer of the largest student organization at Maryland's campus, and had a feel for numbers, but I had no idea what a spread sheet was or double entry bookkeeping.

Imagine my surprise when I found I was the only one in that room offered a job by the Federal Reserve. I asked why me, I had no accounting degree. The reply, "We will teach you accounting." And what a job, I was to be a bank inspector. I would enter a bank without notice, close the bank with all remaining at their stations, and do an impromptu audit to see if all was correct. The dream job for any new banker.   But I declined since I had decided to enter the Peace Corps.

Back to New York and Dean Whitter. Based on my impressive test scores the firm was prepared to hire me. I

then spent three months studying for the next big test
hurdle, the much-feared New York Series 7 Exam, the door
to being a stock broker. While studying for the exam I read
of how the authorities had arrested a group that was taking
the exam for newcomers for an exorbitant fee. This test
was the rite of passage into the hallowed halls of Wall
Street.

Well I delivered. Dean Whitter had not seen a Series 7
score as high as mine, 95, in some time. I was in. But the
next step, real training in what to do, instead of abstract
rules and regulations controlling this pinnacle of the finance
world, was a drudge. I was to sit in a room full of brokers
making endless blind calls to find clients. Imagine sitting
in such a setting from 8 am to God knows when every day.

To be sure I would do this in the hottest office in the firm in
the middle of the dot.com bubble so I would have been
making good money. Dean Whitter was located, as were
most other Wall Street firms, not on Wall Street, but in the
World Trade Center. My office was on the very floor
where one of the planes crashed in the 2001 horrendous
tragedy. When asked what I thought about that horrible
event I reply, "Well I was glad not to have stayed a
stockbroker."

I once more fled this time to a small company really on Wall Street that offered a currency trading platform which was legitimate. It was owned by two Russian immigrants who really understood the business and did have legal access to currency trades. I realized that I did not have the nerves of steel required to actually do trades but instead turned to selling shares in their own trading fund. I recall prospective clients asking me why should they invest in currency trading when buying shares in dot.com companies was so much more profitable? I replied that currency trading did not rely on a constantly growing market but on the acumen of trading currencies at the right moment. Currencies could be rising or falling, the trick was to pick the right direction for any given currency at the moment of the trade.

My advice paid off for my clients. When the dot.com bubble burst they were not affected. In fact, currency trading is not affected by any factor other than which way a currency is headed when matched against other currencies in a given moment. An extremely sophisticated investment but done correctly will always see gains and not losses.

Needless to add currency trading is an obvious integral component of the Global Economy and indispensable for its success.

ENTERTAINMENT

No more prevalent category of goods and services in
international trade than the arts. Top of the list here are
films, movies, flicks, motion pictures. Almost all major
films today involve casts assembled from around the world
supported by writers, producers, directors, technicians, and
of course financiers equally spread around the globe. Films
are a major export for the USA and a select group of other
nations.

Of course, live performances feature international stars and
ensembles. We have operas, ballets, concerts, plays, and
more circling the world with participants from many lands.
Sports also bring players from all over the world to perform
in front of spectators around the world.

Works of art are a staple in international trade. And in spite
of their cost, original works of art usually enter countries
free of any duties.

Hard to believe but movies, concerts, plays, operas, books,
and such all have to pay royalties to the writer or other
originator, no matter where the play is performed, the book
printed, the concert performed or the film seen.

VIDEOS

I recall, while in my second assignment in Madrid, I was approached by representatives of the local video industry. They had a problem, the new Minister of Culture, an avowed Communist, was taking measures to cut off the entry of US videos for the rental business. The most formidable action was to assess import duties, not on the value of the master video imported to make copies for rental, maybe $5000, but on the calculated value of all business done based on that video, i.e. all rentals, that could reach many thousands of dollars. It was impossible to assess such a value, but the Ministry set arbitrary values and the Customs assessed duties based on those values. The new duties made it commercially not viable to bring in the video masters.

What to do? My visitors sought our assistance in raising the issue in our formal negotiations with the Spaniards. I said this would be a long and uncertain process but would put the issue in our normal channels. The subject wound through the process. Imagine my surprise when a short time later my video contacts came to see me to get my opinion on their plan to deal with the exorbitant tariffs.

Ingenious, they had taken a look at Spain's rules for "temporary" imports of goods, basically to bring products in for trade shows and other temporary demonstrations. They said they could bring the video masters in on temporary import, which meant paying a small percentage of the product's full duty. They would bring the masters in for a month or so and run off copies. After that they would reexport the masters, paying a fraction of the tariffs assessed. I said it seemed to pass muster and the video industry in Spain quickly adopted the temporary import duty route.

I learned a few years that we had developed a new plan that was adopted throughout Europe by all video importers. Always good to be present at the birth of a new trade standard.

COMMUNICATIONS

Of course, the service export that has soared to the top of US exports is communications. American business abroad is headlined by the likes of Google, Facebook, and Apple. The world is awash with people wedded to their cell phones, tablets and computers hammering away at messages, usually with photos, describing such critical things as the lunch they just finished or are still eating.

I did not work directly in this mega-industry but did predict it. As head of the economics section at our embassy in Helsinki I was invited, based on an article I had written for a local newspaper, to give a talk to a large group of Finnish businessmen on the state of the US economy. No small task this since it was 1982 and we were in the midst of what many called the greatest recession since the "Great Depression."

In the first part of the speech I boldly predicted that the following year, 1983, would be a great recovery year adding that not many would believe this, but those who did and took appropriate action, would see handsome profits.

Not hard for me to see this since the main reason for the economic slump was the campaign by then Chairman of the Federal Reserve Bank, Paul Volcker, to drive interest rates up to record heights in an effort to control inflation, which had reached record levels for the 20th Century. Mortgages were going for as much as 13% interest. The resulting across the board high interest rates had sunk the housing and auto markets and with this the rest of the economy. Then President Ronnie Reagan countered the slump with tax cuts and "supply side economics." But he knew he had to end the high interest rates and was constantly pleading Volcker to do so.

Just as I was giving my speech in Finland, Volcker dropped the Fed interest rate instantly driving down all interest rates. The response was immediate. The following year, 1983, saw one of the greatest recoveries in US history. Again, not hard to understand. New housing starts in 1982 were about one million new homes built. In 1983 that number doubled to over two million new starts. When the US housing market doubles, you can be sure the entire economy will grow fast.

In a curious note the following year we had the chief economist of the US Chamber of Commerce give a talk to a Finnish group. He was touting the great recovery underway in the USA. He cited the same event, as did I, as the beginning of the recovery, Volcker lowering the Fed interest rate. However, in line with standard "supply side economics," he said it was the resurgent investment that followed the Fed action, that produced the booming economy. I differed since I said it was the doubling of housing sales. We were both right because, while I called home purchases consumption, he called home sales an investment.

The other, more profound, prediction I made in that speech in Helsinki was to announce that the main motive force for economic growth in the world had changed. I noted that for the century up to 1982 the main stimulus for economic growth around the world had been transportation, best seen in our having sent men to the moon. In that hundred-year span we witnessed the growth of the railways spanning continents followed by airplanes that could reach any corner of the globe. And all this exceeded by the motor vehicle, the device that allowed the average man to go anywhere he wanted, at any time, at an affordable price. As proof of my statement that transportation had been the main force behind the remarkable economic growth of the century up to 1982, I noted that, at that time, the largest companies in the world were auto makers and petroleum companies that supplied the fuel for the vehicles.

I went on to say, however, that transportation would be replaced by another sector of our economy for future growth - communications. Many countered by saying, no it was computers. I replied by saying the computer is a tool, not an end-in-itself. And yes, computers would play a key role in the growth of communications. But it was the desire to talk to anyone, anywhere that would lead the way.

I keep a copy of that speech locked up with my most important papers for even I am amazed at how accurate my prediction proved to be. Google, Facebook, and Apple have replaced Ford, GM and Exxon as the largest companies in the USA. Communications have replaced transportation as the key stimulus to economic growth.

WINE, WOMEN AND SONG

WINE

I retired from diplomacy after 25 years to enter private business. You see, an old friend from Turkey, where I had been our commercial attache, invited me to dinner at his US home in Washington DC, my hometown, where I was visiting family. We talked about his latest venture, a joint venture with America's oldest and best-known public relations company, Hill and Knowlton. I told him that it was the right moment to start this kind of business in Turkey. He stopped me in my tracks by saying, "I don't want your advice this time Leo, I want you to run the company." One year later I was retired from State and running the company in Turkey. But more on that under foreign investment.

From that initial experience I went on to work in several industries involved in the global economy.   After public relations I worked with restructuring a fish processing operation in Mozambique, helped establish a black owned commercial property development in Johannesburg, built the South African Trade Centre in Orlando, Florida, was a Wall Street stockbroker in New York City specializing in foreign currency exchange, made clothing for young women in London, England, imported wine into Washington DC, sold Florida property to foreigners, and set up a tour company in Spain.

The most fun I had was in the wine business and why not? Everybody in this business is having fun. I backed into the business when I returned to the USA from having managed the clothing firm in London. I brought back with me two new products to import, the only whiskey made in Wales and a new packaged cocktail from the same firm based on vodka, also made in Wales. The packaged cocktail was intriguing since it was bottled in aluminum bottles with screw tops which were totally new to the market. I thought, the package alone would make it an instant success.

I wanted to import the products but did not want to open a new import business. So, I turned to an old friend and her business partner who had an import business in the Virginia suburbs of DC. They accepted adding alcoholic beverages to their import business.

Little did we anticipate how difficult it would be. We had to obtain liquor licenses from the Federal government and the state government. I was surprised when we were told we had to have an "import" license for Virginia. I asked why when we had already obtained a federal license. I learned that alcoholic products had to have "import" licenses for each state into which they were "imported." Essentially alcoholic products are still traded under the same system in place over 200 years ago, when our fledgling nation was still under the Articles of Confederation, i.e. goods were "exported" and "imported" between the states with customs duties and other controls.

We obtained all the federal and state licenses but it took some time and effort. In fact, as it turned out my strength in the liquor business was that, as a long- time federal employee, I was very familiar and comfortable with government rules and regulations. We literally had a wall full of licenses to import, transport, sell, promote, discuss and more for liquor in several jurisdictions.

We spent about a year obtaining the licenses and making contacts to sell the whiskey and vodka cocktail. We were reaching the end of the tedious and expensive process when we got word from the Welsh maker that he was appointing another importer for his products. We were mad, after all the time and expense, the maker cut us down. I took my revenge. At that time, I was providing information on the company's products to the Bureau of Alcohol, Tobacco and Firearms, the ATF of Waco, Texas infamy. ATF wanted to know precisely what ingredients were in the vodka drink. I replied that the company was not sending me all the details

ATF wanted and I suspected they knew the product would not pass muster. The company would learn that you don't fool with ATF nor with me. It never got approval for its products.

We were left with all the licenses to import alcoholic beverages but with no product. Enter a friend from Spain who contacted me to offer a new idea, why didn't we import wine from Spain? He noted that our licenses covered wine as well as spirits. Not a small consideration since, not all who apply for these licenses, get them. I should also note that in the alcohol trade there are two categories of licenses, those for wine and spirits and those for beer and other malt beverages.

I told my friend that I had no real experience in wine and added that I drank beer. I said we would go with this if he selected the wines and sent us good ones. Little did I know at the time that, while Spanish wine offers the best price to quality offer, it had poor reception in the US market.

To launch the enterprise, I took a table at an upcoming wine fair hosted by the Spanish Embassy in Washington at the lovely building between the White House and the Washington Monument known before as the Pan American Union, now as the Organization of American States headquarters.

I visited the place as a kid (I was born and raised in DC). It opens with an indoor two-story garden, almost a mini-forest. From that introduction follows a series of elegant rooms of various sizes for different purposes. The wine show was to be held in the main salon.

My man in Madrid sent us samples of wine that arrived just before the show. We were ready to go but there was a hitch. The bottles had to have a label showing that they were being brought in for a trade show with certain requirements. We had the labels made and I went personally to the shipping office that had received the wine at the Dulles Airport near us in the Virginia suburbs of DC. I was allowed to enter the customs bonded area and attach the labels. I then formally imported the wine.

But further complications. I could not transport the wine samples myself to the show since we did not have a license to transport alcohol, in fact three licenses, a federal license, a Virginia license and a DC license. We had our freight forwarding agent bring the samples to the show. The result was that we got the wine a few hours before the show.

So, there we were, a few hours before the show and no idea what our wine was like. I opened the ten samples or so and methodically went down the row sampling each wine. At one point I stopped and told my colleagues, this was it, the wine I had just sampled was superb, or at least to my uneducated palate it was.

We put the wine I selected in front of all the samples and pushed it during the show. It was a hit. All agreed that it was clearly the superior wine of our group, in fact it was judged to be one of the best in the entire show.

Spurred by my ability to pick out a good wine I then committed a major error. I ordered an entire shipping container of just that wine, 750 cases or 9000 bottles. All our contacts in the business told me that I should have ordered a selection of several wines, but I insisted we would go with my favorite.

By now my Madrid contact had confirmed my selection by telling me that the same wine had been ordered for the cellar of the King of Spain, so it clearly was a good wine. But still, all called me a bit foolish for putting all our eggs in one basket.

Then the trauma. The wine left the winery in April, at the beginning of the warm weather. We did not know where the container was placed on the boat bringing it to America, fearing that the ones on top got the full sun and, in our case, would have "cooked" the wine. In fact, the wine had to go to England where it was transshipped to a boat to Norfolk, Virginia, instead of to Baltimore, where we had rented storage space. From Norfolk the wine went by barge to Baltimore where the container sat on the dock for over a week because of a strike.

By the time the wine got into our warehouse it had gone through quite a trip. I went to the warehouse to check the shipment. We had not imported the wine, so it was still in the bonded area of the warehouse. I got permission to enter the area and test the wine. I had a cork puller, but no glass, so borrowed a cup from the warehouse.

Ii surveyed the cases of wine and thought to myself, "I could have 9000 bottles of vinegar."   Scared I randomly selected a case and took out a bottle of the wine placing it on top of a stack of cases. With trembling hands I pulled the cork. Trembling even more I poured a small amount in my cup. Then with two hands shaking so hard I could barely hold the cup I raised the cup to my mouth and took a sip. Brilliant! Whatever had happened to the wine on its long journey, it was better than when I tasted it at the show.

We imported the wine and sold it like hot cakes. It was an instant smash hit. We were in the wine business!

SWITZERLAND

From that initial success we expanded to import more wines from Spain and elsewhere. In short order we were importing from Spain, Portugal, Italy, Austria and even Switzerland, in fact we were one of the few importers bringing in product from Switzerland. In our case we imported a "sparkling" wine which we shamelessly touted as "champagne." It was a hit since its price came in under the French stuff and just above the California price.

We introduced the "champagne" at a Swiss products exhibit at the Swiss embassy in DC. I warned the staff there to open the bottles carefully since they packed plenty of pressure. As I warned, the first cork popped by the staff sailed across the entire length of the exhibit hall. The embassy was delighted with the hit of their trade show, "champagne" from its vineyards.

ITALY

Our Italian wine came to us by chance. We were exhibiting our wines at the big wine show in DC held each January in the massive Ronald Reagan Building in the center of the town. I took a break to see what else was being offered. I wandered through the extensive Italian exhibit where I found a wine maker standing with his babies.

I told him, "Okay, give me your best shot."

He replied, "I have a beautiful merlot."

I said, "I don't like merlot, show me something else."

He insisted and poured me a taste. I raised the glass to my nose and without tasting it, asked, "How much."

The winemaker exclaimed, "You want my best wine." "I have to sell my white too."

"I don't want your white, how much?"

Giovanni Fofani and I haggled for a while and came to an agreement, I would have to buy a bottle of his white for each bottle of merlot I bought. He asked me which white I wanted, I replied, "I really don't care." He let me taste a few and I settled on a Sauvignon Blanc.

Some five months later I was in Italy on a buying trip. I had some customers who wanted Chianti. I started by trip by going to Venice where my Italian supplier, Giovanni, picked me and my traveling companion up and took us to his winery near the city of Udine. Funny, my father spent the second world war stationed near there, where he arrived just after the war was over. He had a marvelous time since he spoke Italian and had money. In postwar Italy he was a king.

Govanni's winery was located in an estate that had been in his family since the 16th Century. He had left his banking job in Milan to come with his wife to the family home, a massive farmhouse dating back to the 16th Century, that they had lovingly restored. Even more impressive, he had completely rebuilt the estate's vineyards and a winery.

We arrived and went to the kitchen where his wife had a lunch waiting. However, first we had to try some wine. Giovanni gave me a glass of white which I tasted. "Fantastic," I exclaimed, "what wine is this?"

"The one you bought," replied Giovanni.

"I bought this?"

"Yes, but the sample you tried in Washington was from the barrel, this one has been in the bottle for some months."

So, I learned another important lesson, wine gets better aging in the bottle. It also gets better aging in barrels. In fact, wine gets better with age, but each wine has a different optimum aging time.

From Venice we went to Florence to find Chianti. We were staying in a boutique hotel where I got into a conversation with the manager, a young lady from Colombia. She asked me why I was in Italy and I replied, "To buy wine."

The manager immediately said I had to meet the hotel owners who had a winery. I said okay and we agreed for her to take us there the next day. Next day we were off to the winery. Imagine my surprise when we drove to a castle in the Tuscan hills. There, on the drawbridge over the moat surrounding the castle, stood the wine maker, Count Fabiani. He took us straight to the kitchen, it seems as though all wine makers like to entertain buyers in the kitchen. The Contessa had prepared a magnificent meal and while we dined we talked about Fabiani's wine. He was already selling in the US market but was always looking for more access so we settled on my reviewing his wines and letting him know what I wanted.

The Count accompanied us back to the car. As we walked across the draw bridge he looked at me, pointed to a castle on another hill in the distance and asked, "Leo do you see that castle over there?" I replied, "Yes." Fabiani continued, "That was where Machiavelli lived, but his family and mine were enemies." Wow, history in the flesh.

That evening we went to hear an old friend, Mario Scarpecchi, who played the piano at Florence's "Grand Dame" hotel, the Excelsior. I had met Mario in my days running the PR firm in Ankara, Turkey. The Sheraton Hotel, which featured the only casino in Ankara, was exactly half-way between my office and my apartment. I walked to work so stopped by the casino each night to gamble and feed on the complimentary appetizers. I also began each evening by going to the hotel bar to hear Mario play. We became friends. That was the last time I saw Mario. I assume he is still living in his ancient stone water mill in the middle of his vineyards writing music.

The following day we took a train to Sienna where we were picked up by another winery, this one I had contacted and asked to visit them. We were taken to a 17th Century palace, which was a museum featured in all books about Tuscan palaces and, also, the headquarters of the winery. This time not the kitchen, but another magnificent meal in a dining room that stretched about 10 meters with hand painted Etruscan ceilings and walls. We talked wine. After lunch we were taken to the trophy room with heads of wild beasts from around the world. As we sipped brandy I thought to myself, "I could not buy a trip to Italy like this."

AUSTRIA

On another buying trip to Europe I visited our supplier in Austria. This was a special arrangement. I had been approached in Washington by a representative of the ancient order, the Knights of Malta, the famous order of knights who had saved Christianity from the Turks when it held firm against a massive sea attack by the Turks on their home in Malta. He explained that the order owned some vineyards in Austria where they contracted a maker to produce wine under the order's label. The order in the USA wanted to bring it to America and asked if I could do this. I agreed, as long as the order bought the wine. In the actual case we imported the wine, but the order did not buy. Without this special market we were stuck with a slow seller. I eventually wound up selling our inventory to the Austrian embassy in DC for fire sale prices.

In any case, before we actually had experience with the wine, I visited the winery on the banks of the Danube. Lovely place. It was, however, a slack time and the winery was almost shut down. We started with a discussion of the wine and then the obligatory tour of the winery. If I never see another wine press it won't be too soon. The final part was to descend into the winery's ancient cellars. There I was shown massive wooden barrels which were built in situ, since they were so large. In fact, one could have served as a small apartment.

The treat was the most remote part of the cellars, a huge natural cave with wine stored everywhere. My hosts asked me how long did I think the cave had been used to store wine. I said I had no idea, maybe centuries. Then my hosts wowed me, they said, "this cave has been used to store wine for over 1000 years." I took a harder look so as to etch the image in my mind.

SPAIN

Spanish wine was our mainstay. After our initial success we became rather well known for Spanish wine and we took on new lines. Spain was not well established in the US wine market and our wines did not even figure among the best known of that small offer. However, we made steady progress by selecting wines that offered great quality to price value and that matched the US palate.

There are thousands of wines produced in the USA and even more around the world. They all share one goal, to sell in the US market. We had to examine hundreds of wines to find our choices. All selected had to have great quality and good price, which anyone in the business can determine. Our ace in the hole, however, was that, in addition to these two determinants of a good bet, we knew what would sell in the US market. When talking to wineries about their product I always said, "You know you have a great product and a competitive price, but what you don't know is if it will sell in the USA. And that is why you need me."

We became so good at Spanish wine we were invited to join group visits to meet Spanish wine makers, courtesy of the Wines From Spain Office in New York City. On my first visit I joined a group of ten wine importers in Madrid. Five of the group were Spaniards who had set up wine importing businesses in the USA. Four were people who had grown up in the wine business. One was a rank amateur, me.

Our first stop was in the town of Rueda, in the heart of Spain. We sat for a presentation by the local organization of wine producers. In effect, the wine makers of Rueda had decided to make their town the leading center for white wine production in Spain. Not a hard job since there was very little white wine being produced in Spain except for "cava" or the Spanish version of champagne. In fact, cava was the only Spanish wine that had done well in the US market where it accounts for more sparkling wine sales than French champagne.

From the presentation we went to taste the products of various wineries in the town that were displayed on tables outside the presentation room. I followed the group tasting wine and making comments along with all. I finally stopped at one table and tried their best. One sip and I exclaimed, "this wine tastes like bananas." Knowing that I was the only newcomer to the business, all tried to correct me saying it was the barrel or the grape or the sun set or the moon rise. I insisted in my opinion and imported the wine. At our company in the Washington suburbs my colleagues would joke about my "banana" wine.

Confirmation of my nose and palate came from my "banana" wine. In preparing to show it at a wine exhibition I had to write a description of the wine for the visitors. To write the note I decided to read the materials from the winery. Imagine my surprise when I read that, "In our winery we use traditional methods with some modern techniques. For example, we use, banana yeast." That was it, I had detected the yeast used to ferment the wine. I showed my discovery to my colleagues who were amazed. From that time on no one questioned my selections or my nose and palate.

In another amusing tale, we sold wine to the top Spanish restaurant in Washington, in fact, probably the best Spanish restaurant in the USA. The restaurant was a sister of a famous restaurant in Madrid and bore the same ungainly name, "La Taberna de la Alabadero." Few Spaniards, much less foreigners, know that the "alabaderos" are the king's guard who carry lances with axes, the halberd in English,

known far and wide as the arms carried by the,
"Beefeaters," or guardians of the Tower of London.

The joke was that we Americans were selling Spanish wine
to this Spanish culinary icon staffed by Spaniards. They
used to ask me where I found the wine we sold to them as
one of their premier labels. I always replied, "I know
where to find this wine and you don't. That's why I sell it
to you."

I found the wine they asked about in a cooperative in the
tiny town of Bullas in Murcia Province. Most American
importers will not buy from cooperatives since the winery
has no control over the grapes they use, they must use the
grapes produced by the growers who own the cooperative.
This does not allow them the flexibility of other makers
who can select the best grapes available and thus offer
better products. I bucked the standard practice and took on
products from cooperatives and thus had wines no one else
offered. It took more work to find the best wines but the
extra time paid off.

I should note here that most wineries do not use their own
grapes, except for the small wineries with limited
production. The usual practice is for wineries to let the
growers grow the grapes. Another exception to this rule are
the huge companies with miles of vineyards, who are thus

able to select the best of the best from their extensive grape production.

To further understand the business, one should focus on the fact that French wine makers, and, to a lesser extent, other European wine makers, present their wine as the product of a given region, not the grape, as we do in the USA. Thus, the French product is almost always a blend of grapes, the famous "meritage" or blend. The trick is to insure that the blend always yields the same taste and in this the French are unexcelled.

In contrast, the common comment about Spanish wines is that there is, "a surprise in every bottle," which means they lack consistency in taste. Stark contrast to the most widely sold wine in the world, Mouton Cadet, from the Rothschild winery in Bordeaux, France. The French product has a reliable taste which one can depend on. Of course, the actual quality varies over the years, but the taste remains the same.

I tell people if they really want to learn the basics of wine making they should go to Bordeaux during the grape harvest. They will see French wine makers walking through the fields sniffing the air. They will stop in front of a specific stand of grapes and buy the entire production based on simply sniffing the air. They then insure that they get the right variety of grapes to make their consistent wine.

Regions are also important in Spain but, with standard varieties of grapes, produced in all regions, this is no longer the best test of good wine. In fact, our star wine came from the lowest rated region of Spain, Valdepenas. It was produced by Spain's largest wine maker, Felix Solis. And while Solis makes literally millions of bottles of wine, it devoted a small area of grape production to careful production of the famous tempranillo grape that was made into a premier wine. This was their headliner wine, the one that drew people to their lesser, but more plentiful, and cheaper, products.

No, in Spain the main emphasis is on the age of the wine. The terms crianza, reserva, and grand reserva have meaning and importance. There is also "vino joven" or young wine that is not aged. Crianza stays about 3-6 months in a barrel, reserva at least a year and grand reserva at least three years. The aging definitely improves the quality of the wine. The trick here is to match aging to price but this is no sure thing. A good wine is a good wine and a bad wine is a bad wine no matter how long it has been aged.

I learned a lot about wine and became something of an expert. However, while it is a hell of a lot of fun, it is not the most profitable business.   I moved from wine to real estate the best money-spinning business. I still offer consulting services to wine makers in Spain but usually limited to just determining if their wine will sell in the USA.

I also give advice to friends and others about how to select good wine. For those who ask about French wine when they are going to a fine French restaurant I say, "Ask the sommelier or wine steward for the wine list. Look down the list of Bordeaux wines and pick the cheapest." When they ask, why does this work, I reply, "Because there is no bad Bordeaux wine." For Italian wine I urge them to seek out the San Giovese grape which is the grape usually used for Chianti. And for Spanish wine I steer them to the tempranillo grape and a reserva.

Of all my job titles, I like being a "wine merchant" best.

UKRAINE

While we were fully engaged in importing wine, I did not forget our original intent to import spirits. By the time we got the wine business up and running my wife had moved from her post in New York City to our embassy in Kiev, Ukraine. I spent time at our import business in Washington and at our new home in Kiev.

To put my time in Kiev to good use I checked out the country's wine production and its vodka products. The most famous wines in Ukraine come from the Crimea where there is, near the resort town of Yalta, a winery that made wines for the Tsar. I took my wife on a trip to the town.

I will never forget the plane we had on the way down. It was a prop driven small passenger plane right out of the early days of commercial aviation. We sat in wicker chairs at a small table for our lunch served with panache, just like the images one saw of early flying on old PanAm flights to the Caribbean.

With no real wines to offer I turned to Ukraine's vodka. My first buying trip was to once again Crimea, its capital Simferopol. I spent a day at a distillery there sampling the product and going over contract terms. We tried to import what was a fine vodka but again no luck.

Undeterred I next contacted a vodka maker in the middle of Ukraine's "black earth" land where the black soil goes down ten feet or more and yields the richest wheat harvests in the country. I went down with a group from the embassy to the city of Cherkesy on the Dnieper River that splits Ukraine between its eastern Russian roots and western "Ukrainian" heritage.

The group returned to Kiev and I stayed the night at a hotel there with no English-speaking person in sight. The next day I was picked up by a van from the vodka factory. My guide was a teacher from the town where we were going. For all intents and purposes he was Dr Zhivago in the flesh, slender, pale complexion, aesthetic looks. We got to the factory in the middle of Ukraine, a town whose name I have forgotten, but a cookie cutter Soviet style city that had no commercial center, but was an assembly of homes and industrial parks, arrayed in no particular fashion.

I was greeted at the entrance to the factory by its manager, who bore a remarkable resemblance to Nikita Krushchev, short, rotund, bald, with a wart on his face. He guided me through the factory, which was well laid out but a bit old. As with any vodka maker he crowed about the quality of the water they used which came from artesian wells. I liked the man and found him charming.

The tour ended in their reception room, a wood paneled salon where we sat to taste the products. We were well into our drinking and eating caviar when "Krushchev" said he wanted me to meet the head of their laboratory. All wineries and distilleries of a certain size have their own labs to maintain quality control. In came the head of their lab, Ludmilla who was right out of a poster for the old Soviet

Union women's Olympic squad. My height and weight, 6 foot, 200 lbs, with mustache and shoulders a yard wide.

The scene was priceless, an ornate Russian reception room, with crystal glasses of vodka accompanied by caviar, and Dr Zhivago, Nikita Krushchev and Ludmilla, a movie set without a camera. What an experience. We continued to talk and drink until my hosts took me to the local bus station and poured me on to a bus headed for Kiev.

We continued to correspond but never did import the company's vodka. I did see the manager at a trade show later in Kiev where we had a pleasant reunion. I explained to him that it would cost more money to bring the vodka to the US market than we could afford. He did not take the hint and did not offer to pay part.

No matter, my visit to the factory was a very memorable experience and will always be my main recollection of Ukraine.

WOMEN

Perhaps the strangest business in which I found myself was the making of clothing for young ladies in England, which one friend summed up by saying, "Leo you would do anything to get into women's clothing."

I had a friend in South Africa who was the country's largest clothing maker. She finally closed up shop and moved back to England when the winds of change blew through her factory. It seems her entire work force went on strike and defied any efforts she made to come to an agreement. Rather than argue further she simply locked the front door and walked away.

Fortunately, she had transferred much of her wealth to England and went back there to live. She was doing well until she decided to get back into making clothing. She got the Welsh government to put up most of the money to establish a clothing factory in Wales. I suspect she pictured herself as becoming the Laura Ashley of women's clothing. (Laura Ashley was the divorced Welsh mother who started out in a tent making home fashions that grew into an international concern.)

Unfortunately, the business faltered. The main problem was that she could not find seamstresses in Wales and had resorted to bringing Pakistani men skilled in making clothes from London's east end to Wales where they worked in her factory and lived in dormitories she provided. The business still didn't make it.

On a visit to London I looked her up and talked to her about her business. I agreed to help make it a going concern. I dove into the world of fashion, specifically fashion for young ladies. I learned about the business. The most interesting fact I learned was that young ladies in England spend more than half their income on clothing and accessories. A lucrative market to say the least. I also learned all about the making and marketing of clothing. I finally earned my spurs in the "rag trade."

To show off how much I learned I always ask women what is the most important thing in buying a new article of clothing? They usually reply, "style, material, or price." I then say, "No, fit." The garment has to fit right or the lady will not buy it.

During my crash course in women's clothing my friend took me to Paris to attend the famous fashion shows there. I remember the first one I went to, it consisted of several buildings with hundreds of vendors selling everything from materials to designs to machines. All the best-known fashion houses were there with the endless parades of models showing off the latest designs. I even went to one show featuring clothing of the future and, believe me, the designs shown went way beyond the limits of the minds of we mere mortals.

She also took me to the hallowed grounds of the best know courtiers, the cream of haute couture. I tried to maintain an interest but did not do the exposure I got real justice. I did, however, learn that, what one sees in this year's fashion show in Paris, is for the coming season. By the following year the fashion is all around the world.

After learning the trade and taking a good look at my friend's operation I told her that she had to chuck producing the garments in Wales and source offshore. She resisted since that meant losing substantial control over the production, having the workers under your own watchful eye is far better than relying on someone in another land trying to make your designs. However, I prevailed and, as a test case, convinced her to make her best idea for the coming season, a light jacket made of suede, in Turkey.

I wrote to a business contact in Istanbul asking if he knew of a good clothing manufacturer to make our products. He replied, "Funny you should ask me, I have just gone into the clothing business and can supply your needs." I am sure he got into the business when he received my letter since until then he had been an engineer involved in building factories.

We went to Turkey where we surveyed my friend's facilities, not his, but working through him. My English friend sat down with the seamstresses to see if they could do what she needed done. I learned an interesting fact. Since leather is a relatively expensive material to use for clothing, the pieces are usually butt stitched which means piece sewn against piece, not the usual overlap of cloth. I saw in operation the special sewing machines that did the intricate stitch needed to do this job.

We then sat down to negotiate our working agreement. The two sides reached what they thought was a sound arrangement, however, I protested that there was some misunderstanding that could ruin the deal. They overruled me and agreed to an initial order.

We went back to London to pursue other ideas. Next we went to Portugal where I attended a trade show for shoes courtesy of the Portuguese Government. We took advantage of the trip to visit some Portuguese clothing manufacturers. It was during this visit I came across the machine that made the "endless T shirt." What it was, was a complex machine that made a continuous tube of cotton cloth. To make the shirts the tube was cut into pieces and sleeves attached. Simple. My English friend gave an order to the Portuguese.

Back in London we began selling the Turkish made suede jacket. We called on several stores selling fashion for young ladies. I only remember two, River Island and Jane Norman. I made an offer to Jane Norman at a price my colleague said the chain would not accept. I defended my offer by saying it was the lowest price at which we could make a profit. I was right, the store made an initial order which we sent on to the factory in Turkey and waited.

Our order finally arrived from Turkey just before the Christmas season. My friend cried out in horror when we opened the boxes. The garment was a tight-fitting suede jacket with an enormous fluffy collar made of sheep skin. But the collars fitted were not big enough, fluffy was more like frilly. What to do?

We located suitable sheep skins in Bristol, England and brought them to London. My colleague and I then worked on the garments, me removing the useless collars and she cutting the new collars from the sheepskins. She then found a shop to sew on the new collars.

Time was short. The shop finally had the job ready on a Friday afternoon. We picked them up with a little over an hour before the warehouse, where we were to deliver the order, was to close for the weekend, thus canceling our order. I drove from the East End across London to Shepherd's Bush like a madman arriving with minutes to spare. Anyone familiar with London traffic will realize that that was an almost impossible feat.

All came right, however, when a few nights later we were strolling in Knightsbridge, where my friend had her home, looking for the closest Jane Norman shop. There it was, our jacket was the centerpiece in the shop's display for Christmas!   We had done it.

I returned to the USA feeling proud of my success in the "rag trade." I left my friend with her new business built on outsourcing production. At last report she was still making her clothing abroad, but at that time in Vietnam and Morocco.

SONG

My direct contact with international trade in the arts came via the stage. I had the pleasure of singing in a few shows in several countries. Each show had to pay royalties to the copyright owners. My best performance was a prime example of a royalty payment.

I was living in Windhoek, Namibia where my wife was stationed at our new embassy there. Since I was now in private business I traveled to Johannesburg and other nearby countries to pursue business opportunities. I arrived back in Windhoek one night where my wife greeted me by saying I had to fill a role in a new musical production being produced by the music director at the German high school in the middle of Windhoek.

The school was in the area of downtown Windhoek that still retained the look of the old German town that the Germans lost to the English ninety years before we lived there.

Indeed, there was still a sizeable German community in the town. In fact, you could go to any place in Namibia and find someone who spoke German. My most memorable image of the town was one Christmas night we went to midnight mass at the impressive Lutheran Church that towered over the middle of Windhoek. Imagine entering such a church on Christmas night greeted by the congregation singing "Silent Night" in German. And this at the bottom end of Africa.

I arrived at the school and went to the music room where I found a man seated at a piano.

I asked, "Wolfgang?"

He replied, "Herr Cecchini?"

He continued, "Do you know the music?"

I replied, "Doesn't everyone?"

Wolfgang said, "Not here."

I then asked, "Let me get this straight, you are planning to put on 'Jesus Christ Superstar,' in a small town (about 100,000) at the end of Africa?"

"Ya" replied Wolfgang.

I then cautioned, "The role calls for a bass and I am a baritone."

"We can work with this," noted Wolfgang.

So, there I was, cast as Caiaphas, the head priest and villain of the work. I asked Wolfgang how he had arranged to do the show. He explained that he had bought the rights from Andrew Lloyd Weber's company to perform the show with one proviso, he had to have a multiracial cast, which was a no brainer, since how else would he be able to do this in a small town at the bottom of Africa.

I showed up for rehearsal where a woman with a magnificent voice was singing one of Mary Magdalene's tunes. I was a bit cowed by the prospect of performing alongside such talent. But what fun. It was probably my most memorable experience in cross cultural interrelations. I was the only native speaker of English in the entire cast. Mary was Wolfgang's wife, Jesus and Judas were what were classified as "coloreds" under the Apartheid regime, Pontius Pilate was an Ovambo, the largest ethnic group in the country, and King Herod was an Afrikaner. Other notables were from the German community. The orchestra and chorus were drawn mainly from the high school. The

rock band was a local mixed-race group. And the corps de
ballet was a veritable cross section of nations

We worked hard and put on what was at that time the most
spectacular musical show ever put on in that small corner of
Africa. It was the event of the year and the entire town
came to see it.

After our performance one night we invited the manager of
the local bank, that had funded the venture, and his staff to
a small party after the show. Imagine my surprise when the
manager raised his glass to toast me, "The man with the
deep voice." I smiled at Wolfgang, since I had been his
problem performer for much of the time. I do not read
music, but simply repeat what I hear and have no idea what
the director means when he asks me to hit a different note
or key or pitch.

Even more memorable was our last night. Before going on
stage Wolfgang reminded all to not forget to pick up their
envelope.

I asked some others, "What envelope?"

 "Leo, our pay."

I was stunned, until then I had no idea we were to be paid.
When I came off stage at the end of the show a couple of
my colleagues proclaimed, "That was your best

performance!" To which I replied, "If I had known before that I was going to be paid, I would have been singing like a canary."

I continue to sing occasionally in Broadway shows, the most recent being the spring of 2019 when I sang in "Godspell." I even sang in the opera, "Tosca," with the Naples Opera - Naples, Florida that is.

TRADE HEADLINES

NIXON IN CHINA AND PETROLEUM

I came back from Vietnam to the State Department where I
was assigned to the Office of Economic Research in the
Bureau of Intelligence and Research. Given my experience
with the "Pacification Program" in Vietnam, officially
known as the Civil Operations and Revolutionary
Development Support or CORDS program, I was assigned
to look into how military assistance was beneficial for
overall development in developing lands.

I thought it a good idea to start with a survey of how much military assistance was flowing from which donor countries to which developing nations. I developed a matrix with the main suppliers, the USA, the USSR, Great Britain, France and all the others across the top, and the main recipients in the left-hand column. One could instantly see who were the main suppliers and who were the main recipients and the major flows from one to the other. The paper was based on highly classified sources. However, I managed to get it sent out with classifications in general use. It was an instant hit. Every foreign service post wanted a copy and got one if it had the right level of clearances. It was so well received it got then Secretary of State Henry Kissinger to summon the Director of INR in for a special briefing, a rare call for the INR chief. I accompanied him to see Dr Kissinger who was just as one would expect, not tall, somber face, deep gravelly voice and to the point.

The paper also got the attention of a sister office, the Office of Arms and Munitions Research, that felt we were intruding on its turf. I soon found myself off military subjects and on to the economies of the USSR and Red China. A truly fortunate move since it came as then President Nixon was breaking through the "Bamboo Curtain." I had to deliver analysis of the Chinese economy for the campaign.

One subject of considerable attention was the prospect for
Red China entering the world trade scene. Most dismissed
it as a large poor country with little to offer world trade.
However, I developed an algorithm for predicting Chinese
foreign trade. It was based on the well observed fact that
China had been engaging in world trade through surrogates,
nearby Chinese communities outside China, i.e. Singapore,
Hong Kong and Taiwan. All dismissed my algorithm as
simple conjecture based on flimsy evidence. In fact, after
Nixon broke through the "Bamboo Curtain" my algorithm
proved remarkably correct in predicting Chinese foreign
trade. Nothing worse than being a prophet ahead of his
time.

I then found myself in the middle of another top foreign
policy event, the petroleum crisis of the early 1970s. I
replaced the officer who had been following global
petroleum matters when he left a bit ahead of schedule. I
was charged at first with reporting and doing research on
the nationalization of oil assets by the producing countries,
i.e. taking back the concessions they had given to the major
petroleum producing companies. I believe it was Iran that
started this in the 1970s, although we had the experience of
Mexico nationalizing its oil fields under then President
Cardenas in the 1930s.

The methods followed were a bit haphazard with producing countries at first adopting "salami" tactics which meant taking back the concessions in slices or tranches. When this proved to be too slow they simply seized all the concessions and made agreements for the companies to continue to produce and export the oil for a share of the proceeds.

One thing really bothered me, why did the companies not sue the producing countries for breach of contract, after all, the concessions were assets? But no company tried to get compensation for their loss of a critical factor in their production.

The Middle East oil producing nations lost no time in using their new control over their oil fields by first raising the prices many times the old ones with some oil going for as much as 100 times its pre-nationalization rates. They also used their new muscle to deny exports to the USA in protest of our support for Israel at the time. Many will remember the long lines waiting for gasoline in our stations across the nation.

I was then made a part of a new INR venture. The Operations Center (OpCenter for short) at the State Department is where all messages from abroad first land. The team on duty quickly reads and determines the top items for the day which they turn into the briefing book for the Secretary of State and other top officials. INR argued that this operation should also include all messages from our several intelligence agencies and got approval to provide an INR officer to the OpCenter group. That officer would review all the messages coming from our intelligence sources and add the top stories he/she found to the briefing book. I was selected to be on the first INR team working the OpCenter. We worked in shifts since it was a 24 hour operation.

Given the petroleum crisis my reports on petroleum events were a steady diet for the briefing book. I continued to be haunted by the question about why the companies had not demanded compensation for the concessions they had lost. About the time I left State to go back abroad I suddenly realized the reason the companies were not protesting. As the new owners of the oil, the producing nations could collude to set the price of oil via their organization the Organization of Petroleum Exporting Countries, OPEC, with no fear of retaliation by the consuming nations. If the companies had tried to collude to set prices they would have been immediately hauled in to court under antitrust laws. By allowing the countries to take over the fields, the companies would see their profits go up, with no danger of legal retribution.

Nothing like being the resident expert on petroleum during the greatest oil crisis of the 20th Century.

THE "EVIL EMPIRE"

I was greeted to my new post in Helsinki by a fellow officer who subsequently became a close friend. John Stranford shook my hand while saying, "Welcome to the keen, cutting edge of Western Democracy." You see, at the time we were fully engaged in "Saint" Ronnie Reagan's effort to bring down the "Evil Empire," i.e. the Soviet Union. A major plank in this effort was to prohibit the export of several high-tech products and services from the USA to the USSR. Many in our government were convinced that Finland was providing a way to avoid the bans, with high-tech items illegally passing through Finland to Russia.

As the head of the economic unit in our embassy it fell on me and my staff to continually remind the Finns about our bans and keep an eye out for problems. I exasperated several high-level US officials by steadily maintaining that the Finns were not acting as a conduit for banned exports from the USA and to the USSR. They bombarded me with rumors about the Finns defying our bans.

I received a report that the well-known firm, Nokia, was bidding to rebuild the badly swamped Leningrad (now St Petersburg) main telephone exchange. If they did a good job, they would be offered to do the Moscow exchange, which was hopelessly stymied by an outmoded system, that could not take on any new phones.

The report I received came from another post which heard from the local ATT office that Nokia was offering the Russians the latest technology in telephone exchanges, digital switches. These tiny devices replaced the much larger electro-mechanical switches in all newly built exchanges, something like transistors replacing vacuum tubes in other electronics. Obviously, the Russians wanted the new technology in their new exchanges.

Problem, our bans on exports of our high-tech items included the digital switches. There were some available from other sources, I believe Switzerland was a source. However, the US was the main source of the switches and ATT suggested that the Finns were offering the banned devices to the Russians.

My first action was to visit the Helsinki office of ATT. I met with their staff and asked how did this report get out? The Helsinki staff at first claimed ignorance of the report. I said that was highly unlikely since the Helsinki office must have known about a report on a Finnish project from their sister office. They finally said that they were indeed in competition with Nokia for doing the Leningrad exchange. But they had no real evidence of Nokia using banned equipment in its bid. I ended the meeting by clearly telling them to stop issuing bogus reports.

I then went to Nokia, a company I knew fairly well, since it was one of Finland's largest. I met with their telephone chiefs, who I had met before. I laid out in stark terms that we had a report from a competitor claiming that Nokia was offering the banned switches in its bid for the Leningrad job. The Nokia boys immediately replied that the report must have come from ATT, its main competitor. They explained that they had made two bids, one using the available electro-mechanical switches, and one offering the new digital switches, "if they became available." They noted that their bid was far better than the ATT bid since ATT's bid only offered using electro-mechanical switches.

So, there it was, ATT was trying to submarine Nokia's bid by accusing the company of using banned technology. Nothing more than a panicky sales office seeking to defeat a rival by using bogus reports. I left the Nokia boys with a warning, "If I find you are using the banned switches I will personally come here and kick your asses around this building." And they knew I would, because they had ATT watching their every move.

In the actual case we removed the ban on the switches
before work began on the Leningrad exchange, so Nokia
got the job, as well as the Moscow exchange. The company
thanked me for correctly guiding both sides in a critical
situation.

Next, we got a report from our embassy in Israel stating that
the Russians had a company in Helsinki which was buying
banned US high-tech computers, services and technology
and spiriting them to the Soviet Union in violation of our
bans. I didn't even leave my desk to answer this charge. I
simply responded that yes, the Russians had this company
in Helsinki, but it was selling, not buying, computers and
their related items and technology. You see at the time the
Russians had the best computers dedicated to a specific
task, running totalizer boards at racetracks. No surprise
here since the top spectator sport in Russia at the time, as
well as in the USA, was horse racing. I suggested to the
folk in Washington that they would do well to keep up with
the relationship between hightech items and popular
culture.

Then came the charge from Washington that the Russians
had, using reverse engineering, succeeded in reproducing
Intel's latest and greatest computer chip (the items that
replaced transistors in computers.) Washington knew the
chips were being made but did not know if they were being

produced in series, i.e. in sufficient quantities for general use.

I shot back to Washington a report in which I said if they meant one of Intel's chips designated as something like 8360, then the Russians were producing them in series. However, if they meant another Intel chip, maybe item 8366, they did not have series production. Washington was stunned that I knew the different chips and what the Russians were doing. Of course, I had no secret pipeline into Russian chip manufacturing, however, the Finns, who did have such information, were happy to share it with me.

Then the big banana. At the time Russia was engaged fully in developing its vast gas fields and sought to export gas to the rest of Europe. We were desperately trying to stop this in order to prevent the Europeans becoming dependent on Soviet energy supplies. Our lever to use? We had all the latest technology in transporting natural gas, which the Russians would, according to our calculations, have to have in order to bring the gas to European customers.

In our vast store of natural gas transport technology were two items that were key to the Russian's aspirations for exporting gas. First was the flexible pipe that would be needed in the Siberian tundra where the frozen earth, when thawed in spring, would cause the conventional pipelines, running a couple of meters above the ground, to collapse and break.

The other esoteric US gas transport technology were the devices used to weld the pipes from inside, not outside, the pipe. This was critical since the inside weld was far better than welding from the outside and most safety rules called for the inside weld. To do this we invented devices that looked like submarine torpedoes. The device would travel inside the pipe and at the joints, stop and automatically weld the seam. Some will recall the James Bond film where Bond is sneaking into another country by traveling through a gas pipeline. At one point he is being viciously pursued by a torpedo like device with a wicked welding torch scorching the pipe. Bond escaped being fried by some contrived diversion. The machine was none other than the welding device used for welding inside the pipeline.

We banned the export of flexible pipe and the welding devices from the US to the Soviet Union. All seemed to be in order until I paid a visit to the "Evil Empire." Imagine my surprise when I found two items crowing about Soviet innovations that blew a hole in our ban on gas pipeline critical components. The first paper was about a new flexible pipe being made in the USSR that was precisely what was needed for the pipelines. The second report spoke about the new Russian engineered, and produced, welding machines that could do the inside welds on the pipelines. I dutifully sent the reports to Washington.

The response from Washington was music to my perverse ears. They appreciated the reports which had been confirmed by other sources. However, they wanted to know if the welding machines were one-off items with few being produced or in mass production. I then nailed Washington by reporting that, not only were they producing the welding machines in mass quantities, they had taken out a patent in the USA on their machine and technology in preparation for exporting the machines to the US. The Russkies had a US patent on the machine we banned for export to Russia!

The controversy between our embassy in Finland and Washington over using high-tech bans to cower the Soviets finally came to a head. The leading administration warrior in the program was a senior Department of Defense officer named Richard Pearl, charmingly dubbed the "Black Prince," or some such pejorative name. Pearl pressed for exposing the Finns as subverting our bans to the point that then Vice President George H.W. Bush came to talk to the Finns about the matter.

It was my only time to brief an American Vice President. I met with Mr. Bush for about 20-30 minutes where I pointed out that, if he suggested the Finns were circumventing our bans, they would reply that no banned US items were going through Finland to the USSR and we had not found one case of their doing so. On the other hand, I explained that, if he requested the Finns to not send their similar high-tech items to Russia, they would reply that trade with Russia was Finland's bread and butter and they would politely decline to follow our lead. He did, and they responded, as I predicted.

So how was I so sure that the Finns did not allow any banned high-tech US items reaching the Soviet Union via Finland? To understand this one has to understand that the Finnish government, at that time, and I assume now, had complete control over the nation's economy. Have you ever heard of a nation rationing credit to enterprises? In many less developed nations they ration scarce foreign exchange. The Finns went one better by allocating all available credits to the various companies.

I used to joke that the Soviets would be well pleased if they had as tight control over their economy as did the Finns. This tight control over the economy allowed the government to closely monitor such things as the import and export of US banned technology. While they had the capacity to block any evasions of our controls, they needed a reason to do so. And the reason? The Finns knew that, if they allowed any banned item to reach the USSR via their land, they would lose their own access to our high-tech goods and services, which they depended on for their well-developed industry. In essence, I had the Finns doing the police work and barring any passage of banned items through their country to the Russians.

 On my return to Washington from Finland I was invited to see someone in our CIA. I went out to Langley and was ushered into a room in the bowels of the building. The room was right out of a sci-fi movie with flashing lights, lots of computer screens, and the ultimate in sophisticated computer equipment. I met with the agency's top man on high tech intelligence. He said he wanted to personally thank me for my clear and decisive reports from Finland on the realities of the imposition of our bans on high-tech items to Russia in Finland. He said my reports were most useful in countering bogus charges that the Finns were bypassing our controls.

Imagine, I was the counterpoint to the entire US Government apparatus searching to find evidence of the Finns evading our export controls on high tech to Russia.

THE OTHER CUTTING EDGE OF WESTERN DEMOCRACY

In my initial calls as the new Commercial Attache in our embassy in Ankara, Turkey I met with the Soviet Commercial Attache. We were in a period of exploring a new approach to the "Evil Empire." I spent a fair amount of time bantering back and forth with the Soviet official. I did raise an issue we had, the Soviets were reportedly negotiating with the Turks to trade their natural gas to Turkey for wheat, major exports for both countries. We were concerned that Turkey would become dependent on Soviet gas and thus weaken the southern flank of NATO, where Russkie troops faced the Turks directly in a very mountainous area.

I questioned why the Soviets wanted Turkish wheat when we were supplying all they wanted. He evaded the question by talking about Russia's interest in selling its gas. The only thing Turkey had at the time to offer Russia was its mountain of wheat.

The Soviet official offered to find me some tickets to the upcoming Olympic Games to be held in the USSR. I thanked him for the offer and made a mental note to include the games in my future travel plans.

My dream of seeing the Olympics was cancelled by the Soviet invasion of Afghanistan in late 1979. The result, among other actions by the USA was to withdraw from the Russian Olympics and restrain Americans attending them. Obviously, I had to can the trip.

However, the embassy was still fixated on Turkey swapping wheat for Soviet gas. In a really absurd action our CIA colleagues dispatched people to all Turkish ports to be on the look-out for Soviet tanker ships with gas or oil. I explained to the rest of the embassy that this was not the right response. I said that if the Soviets sold petroleum products to the Turks it would come in the form of crude oil pumped by pipeline from Iraq to the Mediterranean via Turkey. The Soviets would simply check off the oil stopping in Turkey as exports to Turkey. At the time Iraq had earmarked a major part of its crude oil for Russia in payment of massive arms exports from the USSR to Iraq. In fact, the Russians could not readily use the Iraqi crude and were looking to dump it wherever they could.

My boss, as well as the rest of the embassy staff, dismissed my theory of the Russian petroleum to Turkey coming from

Iraq and continued to send spies to the Turkish ports to be on the watch for the Soviet tankers.

I finally won the day when my boss, who was a woman, and I had lunch with Turkey's Deputy Finance Minister, who was also a woman, who my boss greatly admired. During the lunch my boss asked the Turk about buying Soviet oil for Turkish wheat. She replied, "If we buy petroleum from Russia it will come from Iraq via the pipeline from there to the Mediterranean that passes through Turkey." I smiled, my boss replied with a stunned expression on her face.

Subsequently the Soviets and the Turks entered into a major trade agreement under which the Soviets built gas pipelines to Turkey, allowing the Turks to convert from using lignite fuel, the most polluting fuel one can use, and that kept Ankara covered by a brown cloud throughout the winter, to clean burning natural gas.

Always a pleasure to keep my colleagues abreast of what was happening. However, not all liked my corrections and I was often called a "maverick, loner, or non-team player." I recall meeting by chance the head of a sister agency at our embassy in Madrid who was escorting a new officer around the building to meet people. He looked at me and told his new man, "This is Leo, now you may not always agree with him, but never bet against him."

APARTHEID

No account of the major uproar in the USA against South Africa's institution of "apartheid," its elaborate structure to keep the races separated except for working together and shopping or otherwise doing business together, can be given without mentioning the US Congress' "Anti-Apartheid Act of 1986." I had freshly arrived in the Office of Southern African Affairs at the Department of State when I was handed the draft act and asked to opine about it.

I read the draft and made two comments, first, it was obviously designed to show our objection to apartheid but lacked real teeth. The bat contained in the act was a ban on imports from South Africa with some critical exceptions. We would allow the import of "strategic" minerals. I noted that at the time 70% of the total value of South Africa's exports to the USA was one product, platinum, a "strategic" mineral. So, the ban would have limited impact on South Africa.

Having a strong sense of perverse humor, I suggested that, we did not have to enact this bill, but could really make the South Africans fret by suspending our EPA requirements on auto emissions. As I explained, the platinum we imported was the key ingredient in the manufacture of catalytic converters for cars that controlled the emissions. Lift the regulations and South Africa's exports to the USA would tank. Of course, my tongue in cheek remarks were immediately rejected as being "impossible." I replied, "I knew you were not serious."

My other comment about the Act was that one part contradicted another part. You see the Act banned any new investment in South Africa. I said this would completely undermine another major effort under the Act, to foster and promote new business owned by "those formerly disadvantaged by Apartheid," i.e. black enterprise. I said, "How could we foster and support black enterprise if we could not invest in South Africa?" All accepted my position and fell into a quandary about what to do. I offered to rewrite the Act in a way that would satisfy both objectives. I then rewrote the section on new investment to say, "There will be no new investment in South Africa, except for investment in enterprise owned by those formerly disadvantaged by Apartheid." Of course, this raised the possibility of South African companies promoting their mailroom chief to Chief Executive or some such ruse to get by the ban. But my wording was accepted.

My reward for rewriting a part of the 1986 Anti-Apartheid Act was being assigned to our Consulate General in Johannesburg to enforce the act, keep Washington informed of progress under the act, monitor US disinvestment from the country, and, on the other hand, assist new black enterprise.

My reputation for knowing how the act worked spread rapidly and I was answering all questions related to what could and could not be exported from South Africa to the USA. I recall one specific incident when an American, Moshe Doman, came in to ask about exporting steel products. I asked how he came to be exporting from South Africa. He explained, he married a South African and they decided to settle in her country.

Doman's question was simple, he and his partner wanted to export a type of steel to the USA. I told him that, if I recalled correctly, it was a rod that had a screw end on it. He said, yes. I told him to go on and export it, since, by having a screw end, it was no longer basic steel, but a machined part.

Moshe became a close friend. We went to the inauguration of Nelson Mandela as South Africa's first black president together. But more on that later.

The demand for info on how the act worked became so
intense the Johannesburg Chamber of Commerce organized
a large conference on the subject and asked me to be part of
the program. I was to be the technical speaker telling the
audience how the sanctions worked. Next was a professor
from Johannesburg's top university, the University of the
Witswaterrand, known popularly as "Wits." He was well
known for opposing the sanctions and US policy to press
for an end to Apartheid. The third speaker was the Foreign
Ministry's top man for relations with the USA. He also
vigorously opposed our sanctions.

I asked for permission to participate. The Consul General
was not sanguine about the offer since he was certain I
would be sandbagged. I assured him I would only talk
about the actual working of the sanctions, i.e. what products
could and could not be exported to the USA. He passed the
decision to the embassy in Pretoria which was even more
concerned about me appearing on a stage in Johannesburg
to discuss our sanctions. In the end the embassy gave its
approval, providing there would be no press in attendance.
Well I made my presentation which was well received since
it cleared up much misunderstanding about the sanctions.
Of course, my co-speakers tried to bait me into discussing
the efficacy of sanctions and US policy toward South
Africa, which I successfully evaded. However, in spite of

the assurances I received about no press, the front page of South Africa's top newspaper the next day featured a photo of yours truly with my hand in front of my eyes in what was billed as, an attempt to avoid questions.

With the conference behind me I spent less time on answering questions about specific exports. I turned to the matter of US company's selling their investments in South Africa to stop boycotts of their products in the USA demanded by the widespread demonstrations against apartheid. Better to lose South African business, than lose in your main market. This practice was dubbed "disinvestment."

I duly reported each company's departure. It became a methodical, repetitive drudge. To spice my reports I took to giving them catchy titles. "Dow Bows," topped my report on that company selling out. "Kodak's Photo Finish," when it left. "Revlon Takes a Powder," when the cosmetic giant left.

I then turned to compiling the US Government's most extensive and exhaustive compendium of total US companies' disinvestment from South Africa. It became the US Government's standard document to answer inquiries about US disinvestment from South Africa.

As part of my work I had contacts with the Johannesburg Stock Exchange. In my visits to the Exchange I talked to its people about enforcing our ban, which they agreed to do, and the effect of the ban. They explained their creative response to the ban. They adopted a new category of shares that were labelled "S" shares. This meant shares issued after the ban went into effect and thus not open to US investors. However, those issued before the ban went into effect, could still be purchased by Americans. What in effect happened was that US investors were steered to the old shares and the "S" shares were sold to those selling the old shares to Americans. The result is that South Africa continued to finance its business with American participation.

I should note here that the only shares really important for American buyers were South African "gold" shares which, were not investments in stocks of gold, but investments in the nation's core business, the massive gold mining companies. Thus, the reorganization of the market was not very complex, since there were a relatively limited number of companies affected by the ban.

Disinvestment also yielded a famous blunder by our Coca Cola Company. Coke announced that if it sold its investment in South Africa, it would do so in a way that would assist black enterprise. Unfortunately, Coke forgot to check its charter in the country. It was a joint venture with South Africa's giant brewery, South African Breweries

(SAB). This was not a company to fool with, it now owns the Miller Brewing Company in the USA and other companies around the world. SAB is now registered in London and is no longer a "South African" company.

Under the terms of the joint venture, Coke was obligated to give its partner, SAB, first option to buy its shares and SAB made it clear that it would buy all shares Coke sold. Coke was left with a serious PR problem, as well as the US Government, which had loudly lauded Coke's progressive move.

To salvage its image Coke struck a deal that would respond to its promise to disinvest in a way that would benefit black enterprise. It was working with a small group of blacks who had funds to buy a company that bottled coke products in the town of East London.

One of the buyers was a close friend of mine and he had me advising him on what to do. The entire group was, if memory serves me, five black entrepreneurs. My friend, a black man with a most Afrikaner name, Cyril Kobus, was the brilliant manager who had turned South African soccer into the only profitable professional sport in the country.

I met Cyril when he came to see me at the consulate about his plan to buy the country's premier sports facility, Ellis Park Stadium, in Johannesburg. But more about that later.

Back to Coke. I worked with the group in its successful purchase of the bottling plant. It was a success because the new owners did not change a thing at what was a going concern. Rather, they used it as a base to build the first black owned conglomerate in South Africa. And this was all before the end of Apartheid.

I recall having a celebratory dinner with the new owners. I asked the group why did they name the company, the "Kilimanjaro Company?"
Their reply stunned me, "Because it sounded African."

Returning to Kobus and his plan to buy Ellis Park Stadium. My initial reaction was to ask, "You want to buy the citadel of South African rugby?" Kobus said yes. I continued, "What a story, soccer, the black man's sport, was going to buy rugby, the white man's sport's most iconic home." I continued, "If that doesn't let the world know that things were changing in South Africa, nothing would."

CYRIL KOBUS

Somewhere in the history books there has to be some mention of Cyril Kobus. This was perhaps the most extraordinary man I met in Africa. In spite of his decidedly Afrikaner name, Kobus was a Bantu through and through. While he counted the Chief of the Zulu, Mangosuthu

Buthelezi, as a close friend, Kobus was not a Zulu but rather a Xhosa, Mandela's clan. He had built the National Soccer League into South Africa's only profitable professional sport. His games filled stadiums with fans. Soccer was known as the "Black Man's Sport," while Rugby was the, "White Man's Sport." Truth is, Kobus' favorite sport was horse racing

Lesser known was how Kobus used his name and position to topple barriers to blacks and other non-whites in the apartheid state. He told me of one time he brought a whole team to Cape Town to play a game. He booked the team into a top hotel. When he showed up with a group of black men the hotel staff told him he had no reservation to which Kobus showed his printed reservation for all the team. The person who did the reservation had obviously thought the group to be white since it was booked by someone with an Afrikaner name.

Kobus asked to use a telephone and called the South African President's Office in Pretoria. After a few words he handed the phone to the manager who after listening instructed the desk manager to register the entire team.

In another high-profile incident Kobus turned up at the Johannesburg airport with a team consistently mostly of black players. Believe it or not, while there were no blacks playing Rugby, the "White Man's Sport," there were several whites playing soccer, "The Black Man's Sport." He was told they would have to board under the standard apartheid rules, which meant after all whites were boarded, blacks would be assigned to the remaining seats. Kobus said no, they all had reservations and would board as normal passengers. There was a bit of discussion until Kobus pulled his trump card, the National Soccer League constituted a major client base for South African Airlines, which the airline could not afford to lose. Kobus and his team boarded as normal passengers.

No, Cyril Kobus was an impressive man who clearly demonstrated what South Africa was denying itself through its apartheid system. His contribution to gaining equal rights for blacks and others disadvantaged by apartheid cannot be overstated. It was a real privilege to know him and one of my most cherished photos is of Cyril, his business partner Steve Kumalo, and me laughing heartily as we watched a soccer match, probably joking about another stupid apartheid mistake.

Kobus came to see me to ask if American investors would be interested in investing in their takeover of the stadium. I said I would send out a report about the opportunity. However, I added that I had an uncle who was a professional boxing referee in Washington DC. He had been involved in the development of the legendary boxing hero, Sugar Ray Leonard, who was from the DC area. I said I would have my uncle approach Leonard about the opportunity, since I was sure he would be interested.

Things were going well when Kobus had me meet him at the well-known Carlton Hotel, well known because it had already broken the whites only barrier and had become the place to meet for the elite of the black community in Johannesburg. I arrived to find Kobus with a dejected look on his face. The manager of South Africa's leading bank, Barclay's, who was a leading light among white supporters of an end to Apartheid, had agreed to provide critical financing for Kobus' National Soccer League to buy the stadium. He had just told Kobus that he had to cancel his commitment since he was providing the Rugby League funds to keep the stadium.

I said I know why he was doing this. He made a strong statement on ending apartheid that was greeted by massive withdrawals of funds from his bank by irate whites. I said he is just shoring up the bank's position with whites since Rugby, as I mentioned before, was the white man's sport.

I told Kobus to go back to the manager and tell him that if he reneged on the financing he would be toast in the black community. Kobus did and the manager came up with a

solution worthy of King Solomon, he offered to finance a
new stadium to be built in Soweto and named, "Soccer
City." Kobus was back in business and happy.

I recall another meeting at the Carlton where Kobus told me
he had found a buyer for the massive scoreboard to be hung
over the middle of the giant field. I said, "Don't tell me,
you sold the name of the stadium to the bank." He replied,
yes, it will be First National Bank Soccer City (Barclay's
had changed its South African bank's name recently).

Soccer City was built between Soweto (the city for blacks
near
Johannesburg) and Johannesburg in an effort to show the
changing nature of the country. Many will have seen it
when Nelson Mandela made it his venue to speak to the
nation on his first visit to Johannesburg after being released
from prison. It is still there.

BLACK ENTERPRISE

My work with Kobus, his Kilimanjaro group, and other new
entrepreneurs from the ranks of those, "Previously
disadvantaged by apartheid," led me to write another
compendium on a topical subject, the extent of black owned
enterprise in the waning days of apartheid. My ambassador

was aghast at the report since he viewed it as something of a defense of the South African order, i.e. black men are not disadvantaged by apartheid. I said, no, it was a report as I had done with the "Disinvestment Report" based on actual experience. I gave a full account of almost every fledgling black owned enterprise in the country at that point. My intention was to show that, contrary to the line used by whites, "Blacks are not able to create and run new enterprise," black entrepreneurs were already showing they were ready for the end of apartheid and the freedom to engage in any business.

In my report I talked about the Soccer League and Kilimanjaro, as well as the highest ranking black in the insurance business, Sam Alexander, who was another close personal friend, the first black motorcycle cop who opened a delivery system that was growing like a weed, the richest man in Soweto who started as a butcher, and others. It became another benchmark work on the demise of apartheid.

My knowledge of the black business world got me an invitation to attend a meeting held by a large group of black, brown, yellow and other nonwhite businessmen. They told me that the American Chamber of Commerce in Johannesburg had offered to finance a group of them to visit the USA as a "trade and investment" mission. They asked me to assist them in this daring enterprise. I replied, "I will help you with two conditions, you say nothing of my work to anyone at the American Mission (the embassy and the consulate) and you take my good friend Steve Nxumalo (pronounced Kumalo) with you." They agreed.

The reason for my first condition was to avoid the embassy and consulate interfering in what was beyond their ken. I did not need endless dialogue with Washington about the mission. If the American Chamber of Commerce was going to pay the freight, the least I could do was to help arrange the mission.

As for my second condition, the leader of the group, Sam Alexander, who had impressed me when he came strutting into the meeting dressed in a tuxedo with a martini in his hand, it seems he had left a party to attend the meeting, asked me why I insisted on my friend Steve being part of the mission. I replied, because Steve is black and the rest of you are classified as colored. Sam was impressed by my knowledge of the apartheid system, enough to know who were classified as being "colored" and those being classified as "black" among those who were in attendance, but more importantly, the group chosen to go on the mission.

For my part I got one of the Deputy Assistant Secretaries of State, Bill Robertson, to make arrangements in the USA for the mission. Bill and I had worked together to broker the first American investment in Mozambique when I was in the Office of Southern African Affairs. But we will leave this for later.

The group was to start in New York City, then Washington and end in Atlanta, Georgia. I saw them off. Bad start. I got a frantic call from Sam and Steve from New York. It seems the African National Congress, Mandela's ANC party, representative in New York had met with the mission and demanded they return immediately to South Africa. He warned that they were being used to soften opposition to apartheid.

Of course, this was pure fantasy, by the time the mission went to the USA, it was obvious to all that apartheid was ending and it only remained to make the historic change as smooth and easy as possible. I told Sam and Steve to take the group to Washington where Bill Robertson would personally meet them and was arranging meetings for them with US businessmen. I then called Bill and told him he had to deliver a good reception in DC.

The group went on to DC where they were greeted by Bill and the DC Chamber of Commerce which did a bang-up job of making them feel welcomed. It helped that most of the DC Chamber were also black entrepreneurs. I talked to Sam and Steve who were very happy with the results in DC.

If DC was a success, Atlanta was a triumph. The host for the mission there was the US Chamber of Black Enterprise since Atlanta was their headquarters. Not only did the mission members get to meet with US investors and traders, the national chamber got them into the Democratic National Convention that was being held there when the group arrived.

On its return to Johannesburg my colleague, the Commercial Attache, held a lunch for the group. Our ambassador attended. During the lunch Sam Alexander raised a toast, the man always looked best with a drink in his hand, to me for having had faith in the mission and worked hard to make it a success. I believe the ambassador finally dropped his image of me as an apologist for the South African government.

Evidence that the ambassador had finally come to understand my knowledge of the black community, particularly the business community, came a while later when the embassy called me to ask that I arrange a meeting for the ambassador with Winnie Mandela. The reason for the meeting was that Winnie controlled who got to see

Nelson, who was still in prison, and the ambassador wanted
to make a pitch to see Nelson. I replied, "why me, given I
was not at the embassy but at the consulate in
Johannesburg?" I did not also say, "Why me when the
ambassador thinks I am a closet supporter of the
government," rather I continued by saying, "I will do it, but
with one condition, the ambassador meet with the Soweto
Chamber of Commerce."

The ambassador came for the meeting. I took him to the
Soweto Chamber where its president made it clear he
looked forward to many contacts with American business
and hoped the ambassador would do what he could to
encourage American firms to consider investing in black
owned enterprise in South Africa.

The Chamber President then escorted our small group from
the mission on a tour of Soweto. At one point we stopped
our cars and the Chamber President's right-hand man, Gil
Kaba, got out. He entered a standard Soweto small red
brick home and came out with Winnie Mandela dressed to
the nines, you see, Gil was Winnie's brother-in-law. The
ambassador had his meeting on the sidewalk in front of the
house. After an exchange of pleasantries, the ambassador
made his request to meet Nelson. Winnie agreed to
consider it.

On our return to our cars the ambassador, who was
obviously excited with his visit, said it had been an
excellent exchange. I replied all that happened was for him
to ask to see Nelson. He continued by saying they had
discussed several important issues. I took the hint and on
return to the consulate wrote an almost poetic serenade
about the seminal meeting between our ambassador and
Winnie Mandela. It flew to Washington.

Still another part of the Anti-Apartheid Act called for our
Export-Import Bank, the US Government owned bank
designed to finance major exports like aircraft and power
stations, to provide financing for black owned enterprise to
use in buying goods from the USA. A two-person
delegation from the bank came to Johannesburg where I
was to escort them on visits to potential borrowers. As we
rode back to the consulate from the airport I asked them
about their plans. They said they had the name of a well
established Indian merchant who sounded like a good
client. I replied, if that was all they were going to do, it
would be better to turn back to the airport and go home. I
said we needed Ex-Im financing for new black enterprise,
not to lend to those who already had adequate financing.

My visitors got my drift and asked, "Do you have any such
enterprises?" I replied yes and from that initial start I
arranged the first loan ever given by the bank to a black

owned company in South Africa. It was a construction firm created by several graduates of a South African Government program to provide technical training to blacks. They needed funds to import building materials from the USA. Ex-Im was able to show that they had complied with their mandate to fund black enterprise in South Africa.

I left South Africa before the formal end of Apartheid and while Mandela was still in jail. However, I returned in late 1991 when my wife was assigned to our brand-new embassy in Windhoek, Namibia. I went to Johannesburg frequently in my new guise as a private businessman. In doing so I managed to actually observe the end of apartheid and Mandela's release from jail. In fact, I was an international observer of the election of Mandela as South Africa's first black president. Thus, I had the opportunity to observe up close the entire drama of the end of the apartheid South Africa and the beginning of the new "Rainbow Coalition" government. Moreover, I played a small role in the historic event.

I recall my friend Moshe Doman and I went to Pretoria to attend the inauguration of Mandela as South Africa's first black president. Fascinating group of world notables on the stage with Fidel Castro being the top draw, followed by

Mandela's wife Winnie, and others. Way down on the list was then US Vice president Al Gore.

As we left the event, I waved my hand with two fingers up. Mosche said, "victory." I replied, "No, two years." And two years later Mosche and his family packed up and left South Africa for the USA.

Good to be involved in a historic event.

THE HOUSING BUBBLE OF 2008

Along with every second person in Florida (you need at least one buyer for every seller) I got into real estate at the height of the housing bubble in 2003. My niche was selling Florida property to buyers abroad, mainly Ireland. Few will readily remember that this was the news of the day. Sunday newspapers would carry three sections of homes for sale. You could sell a shack next to the swamp for big bucks.

What was the fuel for the fire? No, it was not homeowners trading up for larger digs. The impetus came from millions of middle-class folk trying to reach the ranks of the rich off of quickly buying and selling homes in the rapidly rising market. The term used to define this practice was "flipping." With property rising in value by as much as 25% a year in South Florida we were ground zero, outside of California, for this boom market, one could buy a house today and sell it next week for a quick 10% gain.

Buyers were aided in this fast buck market by three facts:

First, one could leverage this "investment," with as little as zero percent down loans.

Second, there is no capital gains tax to pay when you sell your residence.

Third, the Fanny Mae concept for expanding available funds for mortgages was being used by others, as well as Fannie Mae.

I should explain each of these. In stock market and bond buying one is not normally allowed to leverage his investment, i.e. pay with a down payment and a loan. This was severely curtailed following the "Great Depression" of the 1930s when investors were buying stocks with small down payments. When the stock market tumbled in 1929 there were thousands of investors left with loans they could not pay, in effect bankrupt, which led to a sharp, more aptly disastrous, downturn in the economy. To avoid similar catastrophes in the future the Feds adopted laws limiting buying stocks and bonds through leveraging. An investment in a home, however, allowed large leveraging, as little as 5% down payment.

Under US tax law one is allowed to sell his own home for a profit that is not subject to capital gains tax up to certain maximums, that cover most private residences. You can take advantage of this rule every three years. No other investment allows you to do this. One must pay capital gains tax on the sale of any asset they own other than your own home.

Perhaps the most compelling reason to buy homes for resale was the ready availability of mortgages produced by bundling mortgages into bonds to sell to investors. A practice invented by the quasi-private, US Government funded firm, Fannie Mae. The concept was straight forward, Fannie Mae would buy mortgages from banks that it would bundle into bonds it sold to investors. The benefits here were twofold, first by bundling the mortgages into bonds to sell to investors the risk was spread out over many investors, so that a default would not hit any one investor too hard. Second, by buying the mortgages from banks this gave the banks more funds to lend for mortgages. That rare occasion when the Federal Government had a brilliant idea to stimulate the economy.

The market was humming until the real estate market started to taper off due to home prices rising far above the ability of buyers, even armed with plentiful loans, to buy. Happy days were gone again. A bad situation but it was made even worse by young money managers working the market. They made two dreadful mistakes.

First, since the bundled mortgages were not sold on an open market as are stocks and bonds, they had no market to which to value the bonds. Instead they used algorithms tied to the real estate market itself to value the bonds. In other words, the bonds were not valued to their intrinsic value, the return of the bond over the life of the loan, but to an exogenous factor.

The second tragic mistake was that those valuing the bonds forgot that a home is both a place to live and an investment. Being from the investment side of the equation they turned to seeing a declining real estate market leading to homes being "underwater" or worth less than the mortgage held on them. As would any good investor, when he sees the investment falling in value, he sells to limit his losses However, the young wizards with their blackberries forgot that a home is where one lives, so there is another more important reason to hold the asset with declining value.

Proof of their error came when the massive foreclosures predicted by the "wizards" did not materialize in 2008. The annual foreclosure rate in the USA in 2006, 2007 and 2008 was the same, 2 percent of all mortgages. However, the financial panic of 2008, caused by the poor valuation of the mortgage bond market, led to general panic in 2009 that caused the overall economy to tank, with a major result being that some 9 million lost their jobs. While in 2008 one had a choice, to sell his home to stop going underwater or keep it since it was where you lived, by 2009 this choice was gone since you were unemployed. The massive unemployment of 2009 did cause a smart rise in the foreclosure rate from 2 to 4 percent or a doubling in the rate of foreclosures.

Many ascribe the 2008 "Great Financial Meltdown" and 2009 "Great Recession," to lax rules on mortgages. Too many loans were given to people who were unable to pay them. Not a bad assumption, given that most of those buying, did not plan to hold the property, but to resell it as soon as possible. I had friends who had leveraged their property portfolios beyond what they could pay.

However, these loans were not, as most media would have you believe, given to poor people who had no idea what they were doing. No, the loans were given to middle class investors seeking to increase their wealth.

Take for example the infamous "subprime loans." They are called "subprime" because they are offered at rates above the "prime" or cheapest rate the creditor offers. A key consideration for offering a prime rate is if the buyer intends to live in the house being bought. If the buyer does not intend living in the house, he may be offered a "subprime" loan, given the implied added risk that the mortgage holder will not be living in the property. No, subprime loans were not given to poor folk who could not pay the loan but to middle class investors who were not going to live in the home purchased, i.e. bought as an investment.

There were other lending practices blamed for the mortgage market fiasco. Lenders were issuing "no document loans" which meant the buyer did not offer evidence of his ability to pay or had a poor credit score from our infamous credit rating agencies. Still another practice vilified in the post "Great Recession" hunt for the culprits were the "adjustable rate mortgages" or ARMS. These loans allowed the lender to raise the interest rate at specified times in the future.

I am well acquainted with all of these practices since I sold property in Florida to buyers abroad. Foreign buyers could not qualify for "prime" mortgages since they did not live in the USA, much less the home they were buying. They could not provide all the documents usually required since our credit rating agencies do not rate borrowers abroad, in fact their ratings are only available for US and Canadian residents. Thus, they could not provide a credit rating, the key document required. And given the very low rates offered by ARM loans, it was advantageous to use them and refinance later.

The result was that all of my sales to foreign buyers were ones with subprime, no documentation, ARM loans, i.e. the "worse" mortgages that were blamed for the "Great Recession." Absent in this accusation was the glaring fact that my buyers were wealthy foreigners who could pay the loans. Again, the "Great Financial Meltdown of 2008" and the "Great Recession of 2009" were the products of young financial wizards making bad calls about the value of mortgages by using poorly based algorithms based on the housing, not mortgage, market.

Page | 145

No, my take on the "Great Recession" stands in sharp contrast to what most have claimed. However, I would note that my view comes from having worked directly in the business of selling property at the height of the "Housing Bubble" in one of the hottest markets using the much disparaged "toxic" loans that are charged by many as having undermined the economy. In my book, direct experience outweighs idle speculation from the sidelines.

FOREIGN INVESTMENT

And now to the subject that I considered to be my most important work in the global economy, foreign investment. Trade in goods and services are the bases of the global economy. However, there is a progression in how one conducts his business that I observed over the years. One starts by exporting his goods from his home country to another via counterparts in the recipient country, importers. When the business reaches a certain level the exporter establishes his own importing business in the recipient country. I would call this a financial investment. The ultimate step is to build your own factory or platform for business in the recipient country, which I will refer to as "direct investment." Of course, this is the typical progression. However, there are other reasons for going directly to "direct investment." Trade in services typically requires the exporter to have a presence in the recipient country since in services are provided by people, not goods in boxes. I will handle this topic in chronological order and by country. But first a small detour.

DEBT AS INVESTMENT

Perhaps the largest amount of foreign investment is actually debt. The USA has a national debt of around $22 trilliion (to get an idea of how much money that is, the entire world GDP, or total output, is about $ 90 trillion which means the US debt is equal to about 25% of the world annual total economic output). The US national debt is held as Treasury bonds, of which half is held by the government itself or the Federal Reserve Bank, in other words to the US government itself. Hard to worry about debt one owes to oneself. Half of the rest, about $ 6 trillion, is held by foreigners, mainly banks and governments.

The important thing to remember here is that foreign holding of US debt is an investment in the USA. It is money the US gets to use for domestic purposes and pay back sometime in the future. To better understand this concept, I always use the maxim, "One man's debt is another man's asset."

Foreign holding of US national debt along with other government to government loans, loans made by international financial organizations, e.g. the IMF, loans by private banks to foreign entities, and loans between home companies and their subsidiaries constitute what is probably the largest amount of foreign investment in the world.

NATIONAL ASSET

I learned about US Treasury bonds and US currency notes at an early age. My father's older brother, Tony, was a deaf mute. Fortunately, he lived in Washington DC the home of the first secondary school for the deaf, Gallaudet, in America. The school as a few blocks from his family home and there he learned sign language and a trade, printing. Printing was a favored trade for deaf mutes because of the loud noise made by the printing presses. It doesn't bother deaf people, so they are ideal for the job.

My uncle Tony went to work for the Government Printing Office, located half block from the family home. He did well and moved from there to the Bureau of Engraving 15 blocks further away. He actually engraved the plates used to make US Treasury Bonds and US Currency.

During WWII he became a designated "national asset." Being deaf, he could not be drafted, but he had a more important job in the war effort. It seems the Germans were trying to undermine our economy by flooding the US with counterfeit bills (given their experience in post WWI hyperinflation the Germans were experts at printing currency notes in huge volumes). Each morning the FBI would pick up my uncle and take him to an office in the bureau where there were piles of currency. He would inspect each pile and toss out the bad stuff.

My uncle Tony told me through my father, who had learned sign language to talk to his brother, about how he engraved the plates and how they were used. The plates were elaborate etchings, to say the least. One would be surprised by how many designs are embedded in the bonds and currency cranked out by the Bureau of Engraving.

 Over the ensuing years I have come to learn much about debt. One of the most interesting facts is that debt, as foreign investment, is probably the keystone of the global economy. I count myself among the few who recognize the valuable role of finance in foreign investment.

PANAMA

I already mentioned the American who invested in a resort in the San Blas Islands off the Caribbean coast of Panama. His resort consisted of a catamaran, several beach, and a combined club-dining room. He was doing well when the war almost broke out between the San Blas Indians and their rivals, the Choco, from the mainland. My American

investor was afraid the war would ruin his fledgling
business. I already mentioned how I got the Panamanian
Foreign Ministry to intervene in the brewing war and save
the day for my investor friend.

VIETNAM

I was two years in the Vietnam war as a civilian member of
the quaintly named, "Civil Operations and Revolutionary
Development" program or more typically, "The
Pacification Program." No, I was not assisting American
investors to start new businesses there, however, I did get a
first-hand look at the devastation caused by war for all
investments, as well as the economy itself. Anyone who
says war is good for business has a lot to learn. Economic
progress is stymied by war. Look at the historic record of
economic progress around the world. The notable downs
are caused by war.

In Vietnam I saw actual ruined foreign investments, mainly
French investments in plantations producing mainly coffee
and rubber. Most do not know that Vietnam is one of the
largest exporters of coffee in the world. The coffee
plantations during the war were totally abandoned as were
most of the rubber plantations. Vietnam lost a valued
source of foreign exchange for its economic development.

Sometime after the war ended, I was approached by a Vietnamese friend living as a refugee in Germany to import Vietnamese coffee into the USA. The coffee industry had been totally revived in the country and it was looking for new markets. I did not take up the offer but know that many others did.

Vietnam confirmed my conviction that war is bad for economic development.

SPAIN

My introduction to foreign investment in Spain came in a very personal manner. At the time Spain severely restricted the import of cars from other countries forcing the public to buy cars made in Spain by a Renault factory in Valledolid, a Citroen factor in Vigo, a Chrysler factory in Madrid and a FIAT factory in Barcelona sold as SEATs, the acronym for "Sociedad Espanola de Automobiles de Turismo."

The Spanish made cars were not popular with the Spanish public since they were older models and expensive compared to what cars were selling for in other European countries. To force their sale the government imposed a very tight limit on imported vehicles, maybe 2000 per year for a country of 35 million people. This made what imports there were very expensive.

An American air force officer, Bert Schader, who I knew, had been posted to the very large US air base on the outskirts of Madrid. However, instead of going home after his posting, he decided to stay in Madrid. Bert realized the profits to be made in selling imported cars so got into the business by selling used imported cars.

One exception to the tight import quota was given to diplomats posted to Spain. After the car had been in Spain for three years the diplomat could sell it on the local market. My boss at the time came up with a very innovative plan with Bert in which he bought an imported car from Bert with an agreement to sell it back to him when he left the country. The profit Bert was to make was so high that he sold the car to my boss for no money up front, in fact no money at all. Needless to say, I took the same deal from Bert and had a very nice BMW to use for three years at no cost to me.

The tight import limitation was constantly attacked as Spain opened up to the world in the 1970s. The companies already in Spain were demanding licenses to import cars from their factories in other countries. Then the big banana, the Ford Motor Company negotiated an agreement with

Spain to build a new factory near Valencia. The core of the agreement was for Ford to export about 70% of its production in the new factory. In exchange Ford could sell its remaining production in Spain and import cars from its other production centers.

When Ford began its work by looking for Spanish investors, essentially large banks, the Spanish authorities objected saying that Ford promised to invest a large sum in the new factory. Ford said it agreed to invest but it did not say it would bring the funds in from outside Spain.

The plant was built and Spain entered the world of international trade in automobiles. General Motors quickly followed Ford and opened a new auto a factory in Zaragoza. Today Spain has Volkswagen, Daimler, Ford, General Motors, Renault, PSO (Peugeot and Citroen), Nissan, and SEAT which is now owned by Volkswagen. It is the second largest auto maker in Europe after Germany. It produces around 3 million cars a year of which some 80% are exported making autos and their parts Spain's largest export. Estimates place the contribution of the auto industry to Spain's economy at about 9% of total GDP.

The Spanish auto saga was reflective of the general development of Spain. I arrived at our embassy there in 1973. After a few months I declared, "this is the best growth market in Europe." My colleagues said I was wrong, it was a backward country with dim prospects for future growth. Most of their thinking stemmed from the fact that Francisco Franco, the "Caudillo" or "Leader," was still in charge. However, I persisted in promoting our ties with what I saw as a major market for US products and investment.

I returned to Madrid in 1983 where I found that my prediction had come true. Spain was by then recognized as the best growth market in Europe. As it turned out Spain's entry into the European Union in 1986 served to speed up this dramatic change.

So there it was, I had personally observed and worked in what was a major success for the global economy. It was my first experience in forecasting what would be a new "emerging economy."

TURKEY OPIC MISSION

I went to Turkey as our commercial attache after Spain where I found a country in a similar stage of economic development. Here was a large population of consumers yearning for everything from soup to automobiles. Unfortunately, as I discussed earlier, it was hampered by the then socialist government of Bulent Ecevit. Economic growth was stagnant and the foreign component of the economy was nearly destroyed. Turkey was so short of foreign exchange it could not import coffee. Imagine Turkey without "Turkish" coffee. As a matter of fact, Turks drink far more tea than coffee and they grow their own tea.

The general status of things sharply affected our trade and investment prospects. However, I remained convinced that Turkey offered a major growth market for us. I was particularly interested in investment opportunities. In a surprising answer to my interests we received a cable from the Overseas Private Investment Corporation, OPIC, in Washington. OPIC is a US government company that encourages US investment in developing countries by basically issuing insurance against expropriation, the takeover, of American investors by host governments and currency shortages that make it difficult, if not impossible, to take out profits from the host country. OPIC also conducted investment missions to seek out new opportunities in these countries.

In its cable message OPIC said it was planning an investment mission to visit Greece, Yugoslavia and maybe Turkey. I immediately sent in a strong message urging that Turkey be included in the mission. After much back and forth messages OPIC finally replied that it could send its advance man to check out Turkey, but he could only spare one day with us. I agreed.

The advance man arrived and I took him on a whirlwind visit to see my good contact, the President of the Turkish Union of Chambers of Industry and Commerce, who would be our counterpart for the mission, and some selected Turkish businessmen, who understood the value of the mission. As he was leaving, I made a bet with him that Turkey would be the best stop for the mission. If I was correct, he would buy me dinner at the restaurant of my choice on my next visit to Washington. If wrong, I would pay the bill.

We pulled out all the stops to ensure the success of the mission. The Chamber Union was the main resource since it agreed to host the mission at its headquarters building where the mission members would have meetings with interested Turkish partners. The danger of trouble from those intensely opposing the socialist government was emphasized by the armed guards the Chamber assigned us for our transport to the Chamber and for other calls.
I met with the group on its arrival in Ankara and accompanied it to their hotel. We had a discussion of the schedule in which I emphasized the full support we were receiving from the Chamber. The mission's importance was made clear by it being led by the President of OPIC.

I asked him at dinner why their reluctance to include Turkey on the mission?

He asked me, "Leo do you know how many members of my board of directors voted to not come to Turkey?" OPIC has a board composed of representatives of all Federal agencies related to the subject.

I replied, "No."

The President then said, "All of them."

I asked, "Then why did you come?"

He replied, "Because of your convincing arguments."

The mission was a great success in Ankara and Istanbul. I had my dinner courtesy of the OPIC man in DC. And I became a recognized expert in spotting new emerging economies.

AIRCRAFT FACTORY

The two men were ushered into my office at our embassy in Ankara. They explained that the Turkish government had decided to build a modern jet aircraft in the country, and not just any jet, but the then top-rated jet fighter plane, the F16. One went on to say he had been chosen to head the project coming from a successful run as head of the nation's largest plywood factory. The other said he was in the USA when WWII broke out. He chose to stay and went to work in the Glenn L. Martin bomber factory in Baltimore. He was to be the head of the technical side of the operation. I joked if they planned to build the plane from plywood.

We continued our conversation and I asked if the plane was available for NATO forces. They said yes, the Dutch Air Force already had several and the Greek Air Force was testing the plane in the USA. I then asked, "Are there two kinds of NATO countries?" Since the answer was already known to all I continued by saying, "then we can build the plane in Turkey."

I prepared a report of our meeting and sent it to Washington as a trade opportunity. And what an opportunity. The aircraft factory would represent a quantum leap for Turkish high-tech abilities. Nothing else like it existed in the country. Turkey would enter the modern industrial world with a roar.

A few days later our political-military officer, the State officer who worked with our very large military assistance program for Turkey, came in ranting about my report. He asked, "Why didn't you show this to me?" I replied, it was not my custom to show trade opportunities to other sections, I considered them to be strictly commercial matters. However, I quickly added that I would be happy to keep him in the loop on the aircraft factory. He told me to stop working on it and leave military matters to him.

My Turkish friends came back to see if any progress had been made on the aircraft proposal. I told them that I had been taken off the matter and they should talk to our military assistance office. They then told me that they had already contacted it but were told to forget the project. They also informed me that our ambassador was to have a meeting soon with the top Turkish military man, the Chief of Staff for all forces. I told them that they had to be there and make the case for the aircraft project. I gave them some tips on how to present their case.

Sometime later my pollical military colleague came to my office again, this time almost fuming with rage. He shouted, "What have you done?" To which I replied, "Done what?" He stammered "the meeting." I asked, "what meeting?" He ranted on, "The meeting the ambassador had with the Turkish Chief of Staff." I asked, "Was I informed or invited? How, would I know about the meeting?"

I subsequently found out from both sides that the meeting was a real hum dinger. The ambassador went with the head of our military assistance group and a few other embassy officers with their detailed plans for assisting the Turkish military. They arrived to find the Turkish Chief of Staff flanked by my two Turkish aircraft friends. The General caught the ambassador and his team totally off guard and he proceeded to say the meeting would be about the new aircraft factory. The ambassador's team quietly folded their plans and listened.

I also learned that the reason our military assistance people opposed the aircraft factory was that they knew the Turks would use all of the assistance funds we gave them to build the factory and short-change the land forces, which they preferred to assist. My observation at the time was that we should let the Turks take the lead in designing their defense forces and play a supportive, not leadership, role.

The factory was built. My Turkish friends told me that they would inscribe my name on the dedication plaque for my key help in making the factory a reality.

I returned to Tukey ten years later, this time as the CEO of a new Turkish-American joint venture, the Turkish office of the venerable US Public Relations firm, Hill and Knowlton. Among other new developments, such as a return to a market economy, I found the new aircraft factory built under license to General Dynamics, the maker of the F16. It was the largest US investment in Turkey and the key component of official Turkish-American relations. It was also the cutting edge of Turkish high tech   The American head of the factory was the president of the newly formed US Chamber of Commerce in Turkey.

In sum my aircraft factory had become the highly visible symbol of the strong relationship between Turkey and the USA. Unfortunately, my Turkish aircraft engineer friend had died before the factory was finished and the original head of the operation had long since been replaced. My name was not etched in the dedication plaque for the factory. However, the American director arranged a private tour of the factory for me. The operation was straight forward, the Turks built the airframe at the factory and then stuffed a complete US made jet engine through its tail into its body. The avionics were also a package from the USA that was added to the plane.

During my tour I asked my hosts if the plane that was next to exit as a finished aircraft was to be taken out through the huge hanger door in front of it. They replied yes and asked why did I ask? I thought it prudent not to voice my concern about their taking the plane out through a door clearly marked, "Number 13." I rather mumbled something about just being curious.

Name plate or not, the aircraft factory was my highest achievement in promoting the global economy in Turkey.

MOZAMBIQUE

I did not serve at our embassy in Maputo, Mozambique. However, I did work on the country while in the Office of Southern African Affairs during the height of the anti-Apartheid campaign in the USA. I describe my work in bringing down Apartheid elsewhere in this book.

I was the economic officer for the office. Our policy in Southern Africa stood in stark contrast to our more general foreign policy of backing "freedom fighters" in Latin America and elsewhere battling against Communist and Communist leaning governments. Our policy for the region was named "constructive engagement" and was the brainchild of the Deputy Secretary of State Chet Crocker. The central idea was to work with governments, with which we had differences, to change their ways, instead of beating them over their heads.

Perhaps the best example of how well constructive engagement worked was Mozambique. At the time the country was rated the poorest in the world, had a civil war, was suffering widespread famine, had a destroyed infrastructure that was not much to begin with, and a real

Communist government. It was being kept alive by the
Soviet Union that was spending the equivalent of over a
billion dollars a year to do so. As its major benefactor, the
Soviet regime enjoyed a tight relationship with
Mozambique. But the US, through judicious food and other
assistance, had managed to get its foot in the door and
launch a campaign to wean the Mozambicans off
Communist aid and philosophy.

A key example of our growing influence came when we
convinced the government to adopt a special law for foreign
investment. I don't like special laws for foreign investment
but prefer that foreign investment be treated just like
domestic ones. However, as a truly Communist state,
Mozambique had a ban on private business, so a special law
was needed. The country had adopted the law, now it
remained to bring American investors to the land. My task
was to find those investors.

Given my work in other countries in introducing, assisting
and clearing obstacles to American investment my office
thought I was right for the job. I began by explaining that
here we had a real basket case, the Four Horsemen of the
Apocalypse - war, death, pestilence, famine - in the flesh. I
said it would be difficult but not impossible.

I studied the map of Southern Africa and noted that all the
other nations of the region had economies based on

extracting minerals, South Africa, Zimbabwe, Namibia (then Southwest Africa), Botswana, Zambia, or in the case of Angola, petroleum. And here was Mozambique with similar mineral resources and no mining industry.

 I sent a cable to our embassy in Maputo, the capital of the nation, asking it to get from the Ministry of Mines a list of the minerals they wanted to develop. I got a long list which I went through checking several items until I got to one that I drew circles around and noted, "this is it." The mineral I chose was titanium. All asked me why? I responded, "I would not know titanium if you put it on my desk, but you can sell every ounce you produce." The response to my comments was a chattering about golf clubs, jet engines, fine watches and such. I corrected all by saying the demand came from our new laws at the time banning the use of lead in wall paint. This was in response to children dying from eating paint peeling off walls in tenements. Titanium was being used to replace lead in paint.

I came across this interesting fact in a circuitous way. I was buying paint for my house in Mallorca, Spain when I found the top selling brand was named, "Tintalux." I asked why the name and was told, because the paint used titanium, not lead.

So, there we had it, we would encourage US mining companies to look at mining titanium in Mozambique. I very soon discovered that a US mining company with an office in Washington DC, about six blocks from me at the State Department, was looking to mine titanium in Mozambique. I went to meet the president of the company, Sam Edlow, whose main office was in Fort Wayne, Indiana, the heart of the Mid-West lead producing area. Many will remember visiting President US Grant's home in Galena, Illinois. Galena is lead ore.

I asked why the office in DC since he hardly needed to lobby the Department of the Interior about lead mining. He explained that his company made the very special lead containers used to transport highly enriched, i.e. very radioactive, uranium. He had an office in Washington to keep close contact with our Nuclear Regulatory Agency and other related government offices.

I said the reason for my visit was that I understood he wanted to mine titanium in Mozambique. He said yes, he desperately needed a replacement for the large volumes of lead he sold to paint companies, as did all other lead miners. He said he was in a foot race with all other lead miners to find titanium and knew that Mozambique had rich deposits.

Strangely, the Soviets and their Yugoslav colleagues had mapped out the titanium reserves in Mozambique but showed no interest in mining them. I guess the Russkies didn't worry about kids eating lead paint. In any case Sam had seen the reports and wanted to stake a claim as quickly as possible.

I asked Sam if he had talked to the Mozambican embassy that was near his office. He replied, "I tried but those Commie bastards won't talk to me."

I then went to see the Mozambican ambassador. I asked him why he would not respond to Edlow's inquiries. He gave a typical answer from someone remote from the world of business, "His firm in not listed in the Fortune 500." I told him that there are thousands of companies in the USA and he should be glad that one had specific interest in Mozambique.

From that less than auspicious beginning I spent much time with both sides bringing them together. The critical moment came when word reached us that the Mozambican Minister of Mines was coming to Washington on a US Government grant. I discussed the matter with our Assistant Deputy Secretary for economic matters Bill Robertson. Bill had come from the DC city government where he had considerable experience in promoting economic growth. I outlined what I had done, highlighting that the minister was a died in the wool Communist and, in reality, did not want US investors in his country. I assured him that Edlow was the right company to do the job. Bill gave me the job of arranging the lunch he was to host for the minister at the State Department.

I then plotted the play. I had Sam Edlow sit at Bill Robertson's right hand. The Mozambican ambassador, who by now considered me to be part of his mission, sat on the minister's right hand. The lunch went on with all discussing Mozambique's potential for minerals extraction. Then the climax, the minister looked at Bill and said, "At your insistence we adopted a new law on foreign investment, but to date we have had no American express interest in investing in our country." Bill dropped the hammer by saying, "Mr. Minister I have sitting next to me Sam Edlow who wants to open a titanium mine in your country." There it was, the minister had to accept the offer since he was sitting in a room full of people with various interests in the event.

So, there it was, I had successfully negotiated the first American investment in Mozambique. I say first American investment since the Portuguese government did not allow American investments in the then colony.

As an epilogue to the story, sometime later Bill Robertson told me that after the concession was given, he accompanied then President Reagan's daughter, Maureen, to the crowning of Swaziland's new king. Since they were in the area, the delegation paid a call on Mozambican President Samora Machel where he held a state dinner for Reagan.

During the dinner conversation Machel pointedly asked Maureen, "At your government's urging we adopted a new law on foreign investment, but where are the investments?"

Bill asked Maureen to let him respond. Bill then said to Machel, "Mr. President I am pleased to say that tomorrow, here in Maputo, we will be signing the agreement for the first American investment in Mozambique."

Completely taken aback, Machel stammered something like, "No kidding," but in more colorful language. The rest of the dinner was spent in celebrating a new chapter in US-Mozambique relations.

The Edlow titanium mine started with a rather novel idea. The company bought an old WWII landing craft to house its survey team checking out the concession they obtained on beach sands near Beira. The theory here was, that if the rebels attacked, the team could take refuge in the boat and head out to sea.

So why were they on the beach? Titanium exists almost everywhere in the earth. However, there are few concentrations of the metal that make it feasible to mine.

The mighty Zambezi River that flows from Namibia, through Botswana, Zambia and Zimbabwe to empty in the Indian Ocean near the port town of Beira, Mozambique carries a heavy load of titanium that it deposits on the beaches north and east of the town. These are some of the richest and easiest to mine titanium deposits in the world.

Edlow became fascinated with Mozambique and started investments in other activities. Sam's son was made part of the official US Delegation to the inauguration of Mozambique's second president Joachim Chissano, who took over when Samora Machel was killed in a plane crash.

In another related story, while working on the mining venture I was assigned to escort a notable visitor to see our Assistant Secretary of State for Africa Chet Crocker. The visitor was none other than the legendary Harry Oppenheimer, the head of the two major planks in South Africa's industry and economy, the Anglo-American Gold Corporation, that mined gold, and the DeBeers Corporation, that mined diamonds. By the time I met him he had earned the informal title of "The Grand Old Man of South African Mining."

I sat with Sir Harry and his team in a waiting room. He asked me what I was doing at that time. I said negotiating the first American investment in Mozambique. "Investing in what," he asked. I replied, "mining." His look revealed what he was thinking, here is a brash intruder in my business, in my backyard. I could also see him making a mental note to ask his team how they let a rank amateur steal a march on their great industrial empire. However, his reply conveyed none of this, he simply invited me to pay him a call when I got to my next post, the American Consulate General in Johannesburg, his hometown.

After negotiating the first American investment ever in Mozambique I was known around the Department of State as "Mr. Mozambique." Who says public officials cannot create a seminal private investment?

MOZAMBIQUE 11

Five years after brokering the Edlow investment in Mozambique I met up with Bill Friedman in Johannesburg. We had met while I was at State working on Mozambique and he was working with a lobbyist who was promoting the country's interests in DC. Bill came from a wealthy family in West Virginia who had made its fortune in the bakery business. He sold the family business and used the proceeds to open a bank in the Virginia suburbs of DC. He soon fell victim to "Potomac Fever," politics, and got into the lobbying trade in which he did well because of his good contacts. I recall one of his good friends and contacts,

Senator Mark Warner, who had his 15 minutes of fame when he married movie prima donna Elizabeth Taylor.

Bill was so taken by my work on the Edlow investment he decided to invest in Mozambique himself. He told me about the business, which was a model for sustainable development. He had built a fish processing plant on a small island about half a mile off the Mozambican coast near Beira. To build the plant he had bought a single engine workhorse plane which I recalled from my Vietnam days where it was used to ferry civilian and military officers around the country. All the materials, including the large freezing facilities, had been brought to Mozambique from Johannesburg by the plane.

The sustainability aspect came from the basic business plan for the venture. The Mozambican coast near Beira is rich in aquatic life due the vast amounts of nutrients carried to the Indian Ocean there by the Zambezi River (see my item on Edlow). Of particular interest are the world-famous prawns caught there. The prawns were so good, each weekend the road from South Africa to Mozambique's capital Maputo, was clogged with cars loaded with people coming to eat prawns.

Bill's plan was to buy prawns from the local fishermen who went out into the ocean in dugout canoes to catch the prawns with nets. Talk about basic fishing. The canoes were nothing more than large tree trunks with a small space laboriously carved out for the fishermen to sit and fish. Bill would then clean, pack and freeze the prawns to send to Johannesburg in his plane. Unfortunately, when the plant opened for business the prawns got short in supply, most likely due to low waters in the Zambezi.

To supplement the slack prawn supply Bill started buying the giant crabs the fishermen would also catch. I say giant since the crabs measured up to a foot across with their pinchers drawn into the body. You could always tell how long a fisherman had been catching these giant crabs by the number of fingers he was missing. You see, the fishermen would catch the crabs with their bare hands and the crabs would react by using their very large pinchers or claws to fend off the attacker. Losing a finger or two to the crabs was common for the fishermen. Bill would take the crabs, cook them, then have his team hand pick the meat from the crabs for packing and freezing to send to Johannesburg.

I asked Bill if he needed my help, since by then I was in private business and based in Windhoek, Namibia where my wife had been posted to our new embassy in what was then Africa's newest country. He said no, he had a full team headed by a Dutch manager who had several years of experience in Mozambique. I told him I came to Johannesburg often and gave him my contact information.

A few months later I got an urgent call from Bill, "Help, help he yelled." I got to Mozambique as soon as possible. Bill was frantic, the rebels had seized the production facility on the island with the workers having fled back to the mainland or taken refuge in the forests of the island. His chief of security, a former French special forces soldier, had managed to flee in the cabin cruiser Bill had bought for the venture and was sitting out of gun shot in the ocean watching the island and reporting on the situation to the pilot who had manage to fly the airplane to Johannesburg.

Our first action was to call on the general who commanded the forces in the area where the plant was located. He was very attentive, since new foreign investment was given special consideration by the government. He agreed to take action to remove the rebels. I am sure that following our meeting the general called the leader of the guerillas and told him to leave the factory or face his forces. By the next morning the rebels were gone, taking with them all the food and fuel in the place, but leaving untouched the plant itself and its equipment.

WAR

I should take a moment here to describe the civil war in
Mozambique. The country got its independence from its
colonial master Portugal as a result, not of the long guerilla
war waged against the colonial regime in Mozambique, but
because of the upheaval in Portugal in the mid-1970s that
saw long-time regime of Antonio Salazar (Salazar himself
was long dead by then) overthrown by a military junta in
the so-called "Revolution of the Carnations." So-called
because the usurpers stuffed carnations in the muzzles of
the rifles held by the army troops sent to put down the coup.
A main reason for the coup was the widespread
condemnation of Portugal wasting vast amounts of men and
resources to hold its colonies in Africa, Angola, Guinea
Bissau and Mozambique. By the time the generals ousted
Salazar, most of the country was behind the coup.

The first move by the new military junta was to declare an
end to its colonial rule in Africa and negotiate ceasefires
with the rebels in each country. Next was to withdraw its
military force and with them came the vast majority of
Portuguese nationals who had, until then, made Africa their
home. However, ridding itself of one big headache caused
an even greater one, hundreds of thousands of Portuguese
nationals flocked back to Portugal from the colonies,

hopelessly swamping the country's ability to feed, house and relocate them.

I was at our embassy in Madrid so had a ringside seat to the action. My future wife and I drove over to see what was happening. The first thing we saw was that anti-class vendettas and rejection of the dictatorship caused massive resistance by workers and most places featured workers who did not work. I recall we stayed at Lisbon's fanciest hotel, since by then prices were rock bottom. But we had to schlep our own luggage.

The hotel, as was the case for most others in Lisbon and environs, was packed with refugees from the colonies in Africa. Imagine a five-star hotel with laundry hanging out the window of each room. No question the new military junta government was faced with major difficulties.

If the result of independence in Mozambique was bad for Portugal, it was even worse for the nation itself. Official independence came in mid-1975 with longtime rebel leader Samora Machel being named by Portugal as president and his rebel group, FRELIMO, being named the only political party in the country. The Soviet Union, which had been giving substantial support to FRELIMO and was one of the first countries to recognize the new nation, immediately stepped in to help the fledgling government.

But a dissident group, RENAMO, rebelled against the Portuguese appointed government and failure to hold an election for the new government. It quickly garnered support from neighboring Zimbabwe (then Rhodesia) and South Africa who saw RENAMO as a means to reduce pressure from their own rebellions against colonial rule in Rhodesia and apartheid in South Africa. FRELIMO had given vital support to the rebels in both neighboring countries. Keeping it engaged with a rebellion in its own country caused FRELIMO to reduce and eventually end support for the rebels in their neighbors.

The war between FELIMO and RENAMO also played out in the USA. I was at State during the Reagan administration's support for "Freedom Fighters" combating Communist and Communist leaning governments around the world. In stark contrast to the general policy, we were supporting the FRELIMO Communist regime, against those who many considered to be the "Freedom Fighters" in Mozambique. I had to answer many demands from our Congress about our apparent contradiction in Mozambique. I used the patented reply, "Mr. Congressman, our basic policy is to contain Communism and there are many ways to do this. We find that working with the government of Mozambique is advancing that goal better than military confrontation."

And our policy was doing precisely that. As I mentioned, the Soviets were spending over a billion dollars a year to prop up its client state, with most of that being military assistance. Ours consisted of food, clothing and medicine. We did not supply any military materials, so our expenditure was far less than the Russkies. In spite of our more modest expenditure, we found the Mozambicans to be ready to listen to us. The new law on foreign investment was a perfect example of this.

Even more germane to my story, I was working in Maputo to reorganize and get formal authorization for Bill Friedman's investment the night of 15 October 1992 when the agreement to end hostilities between FRELIMO and RENAMO came into effect. After having been in a few wars, including Vietnam, it was a very special feeling to see a war end. Remarkably there were no celebrations to mark the event. The only visible sign of peace came the next day when thousands of those who had taken refuge from the war in Maputo quietly packed up their meagre belongings and set out to walk back to their villages.

BACK TO BILL

With the potential for violence ended Bill and I flew up to the production site. Chilowane is a tropical island sitting in the Indian Ocean about half a mile from the mainland. Bill and his wife Becky were building a very large, thatched roof home facing the sea. They were to spend most of their time there.

I met with Bill's security man, Jean Michel, with whom I joked that he had me to thank for his last two jobs. Before coming to work for Bill, Jean Michel had worked for Edlow, the first American investment I had brought to the country. But I did not joke long since Jean Michel, while a small wiry man, was not someone to anger. Bill explained that he wanted Jean Michel to train his workers in how to use guns as something of a local militia and build a sandbag wall around the facility so as to fight off the rebels if they should return. I flatly said, "No. If the rebels return deal with them the same way you did before, scatter the workers, send Jean Michel off in the boat and let them take what they wanted." I said all his new security plan would do would be to insure death and destruction. Bill heeded my advice.

I inspected the impressive facility. It was working very well with a team of workers picking crab meat and packing it for shipment. The only production glitch Bill had encountered was that tossing the crab into the boiling cook pots caused a shock to the crab's system that in turn produced a bad taste in the crabmeat. He found that the best procedure was to drown the crabs in fresh water and then cook them. It seems fresh water kills the crabs in a more relaxed way.

There was another technical matter with which I helped. Bill had some of the workers laboriously sawing with dental saws around the base of the carbs' claw shell to leave a plump pile of meat on top of a pincer. He said the dental saws were costing him a fortune. I immediately asked for a claw and a mallet. I swiftly struck the claw three times with the mallet leaving a pincer with a nice chunk of meat on top. All were amazed and wondered how I knew how to do that. I replied, "I grew up next to the Chesapeake Bay and have enjoyed crabs all my life. I know how to break them apart."

We went back to Bill's office and home in Maputo where we discussed his operation. Bill said that he could not understand why they were selling well but not making a profit. I said he had too many costs and it was a "long way from fish to dish." He also said he wanted to get official certification as a foreign investment. I asked why, since he had a commercial license that covered the operation. His reply set me back for a moment, "Because we want the special tax benefits available to foreign investors."

I should say here that elementary business shows that one has cost centers and profit centers. In the export business the cost center is where you make the product, but the profit center is not where you sell the product. The profit center is where you take the profit. In Bill's case I said the product should go on the airplane at cost and be dropped off in Johannesburg at the final price to his buyers. The difference, or the profit, should be taken in a "convenient place" i.e. where the tax bite is little or none. I said all this takes place while the plane is in the air. I emphasized to Bill that he should not take any profit in Mozambique and thus would have no tax obligations to worry about.

Bill insisted, however, that he needed some other special concessions for the project. First was to get permission to fly the product directly from the island to Johannesburg without having to stop for customs inspection in Maputo. He was tired of the customs officials in Maputo making him go through hoops to get the necessary export permits, causing the plane to sit on the hot tarmac in Maputo where the hot sun melted the frozen products on board. Bill said he was willing to set up a customs office at his expense at the production site to do the job.

Second, Bill wanted explicit permission to buy fish from any fisherman in the country in anticipation of the business growing. Thirdly, Bill wanted to be allowed to hold his foreign exchange earnings in foreign exchange, since most of his costs were in foreign exchange.

I offered to reorganize the business to cut costs and get him his foreign investment certificate. Bill asked, "How much?" I was surprised when he accepted my offer without discussion. So, there I was, committed to staying a few months in Mozambique. Reorganizing the business did not take too much work and I had it done in short order. However, I knew getting the foreign investment certificate would be tough, especially the permission to fly directly to Johannesburg, which all said was impossible.

I knew the application would have to go through a series of government offices so began a campaign to call on each of these offices to explain what the project was about and hoped to achieve. My first call was on what I hoped would be an ally in the work, the Mozambican Office of Foreign Investment. I was shown into a meeting room and told to wait for "Mr. Sambo." Imagine my surprise when in came a diminutive, very black man. Here I was facing. "Little Black Sambo," in the flesh. I stifled my urge to laugh and started to talk to him, when he said he wanted another person to attend our discussion. He then brought in a young

Englishwoman recently graduated from the London School of Economics. The young lady proceeded to rant about the insidious evil of capitalism and foreign investors who cheated locals. I said our proposal was not a cheat and then settled back to let her spew her objections while I took careful note of what to avoid in the application. I left Mr. Sambo and his colleague "Rosie the Red" a little concerned, since I had hoped that office would be my main support in the application process.

I continued to make the rounds of government offices. The climax came in my visit to the Directorate of Fisheries. This would be the key office in the decision to grant Bill a certificate as a foreign investment. I first met with the directorate's foreign adviser, an affable Irishman who was very interested in our project.

We were enjoying a good discussion when the director himself came in muttering about our being illegal. I responded that Bill had a valid commercial license. The director continued by saying we were fishing illegally. I quickly said, Bill's company was not fishing, but rather was set up to buy from small fishermen.

I then asked, "Don't you want to help your small fishermen, or do you prefer working with large foreign fishing boats that were literally sucking everything they could out of Mozambique's coastal waters?" The director said of course he wanted to help his small fishermen. I then said, "Good, because if you had answered otherwise this article," which I placed on the table, would appear in most South African papers tomorrow." The article, that I wrote, started with the headline, "Mozambique Prefers Foreign Fishing Giants to Its Own Fishermen."

I finished the application and my calls and went back to Namibia. I returned to Mozambique when I got a call from Bill to come. On arrival I found that they had received the government's reply on the application which Bill's Dutch manager had received. The manager noted that the approval did not contain the special permission to fly directly from the island to Johannesburg nor the foreign exchange arrangement Bill sought. And while it did give Bill permission to buy fish from anyone in the country, it also committed him to assist in developing the nation's fishermen by supplying them with tools and equipment and financing.

I took Bill and the document to the office that had issued it and which I cannot remember now. I began by saying that the authorization did not contain the special permission to fly directly from Chilowane to Johannesburg. The official stopped me by saying, "But we gave you this permission." I showed him my copy which did not contain the permission, to which he replied, that it was not the final version, and handed me a copy of the final version, which very visibly allowed the direct flights. Bill's Dutch manager had made a terrible mistake.

I thanked the official and went on to say that Bill could not provide tools and equipment for every fisherman in Mozambique. His was a business venture, not a development project. The official laughed and said, "We thought we would try it, but will scratch it out." I then mentioned the special arrangement for foreign exchange, but Bill interrupted by saying he would handle this in another way. We thanked the official profusely and left. On the street I turned to Bill and said, "Well Mr. Friedman you have your foreign investment certificate. Congratulations!"

From Maputo Bill asked me to go to Johannesburg and take a look at his operation there, which was essentially a home base for the airplane and a small sales office. I found a host of major problems with his accounting and banking. I went to the accounting firm which was a major US company. They told me that Bill had ordered them to turn the company's books over to me. I refused to accept the books saying, "I enjoy life too much to spend time in a South African jail." I explained that I had reviewed the accounts and found several serious errors that I would report to Bill.

At Bill's instruction I went to the bank there from which he had obtained a loan to buy the plane. To get the loan, he had to deposit a considerable amount of dollars in an account with the bank. I found that they had converted the dollars to South African Rands which had subsequently lost substantial value.´ I asked about the interest payments being made on the account. They directed me to one of their branches which I knew to be a small operation in a supermarket. I went to the branch office, where I was met by a very nasty woman, who said they had been paying the interest to the wife of the account owner, who came in periodically to collect it. I said that was impossible since the account was in the name of Bill's partner in the USA who had never visited South Africa nor had his wife been there. The branch manager flushed and said let me check this out. She returned to apologize, it seems the bank had been paying the interest to another person with a similar name and she would clear up the mistake.

I then went to see Bill's main buyer who had been buying most of his prawns and all of his crabmeat. I told him we had to raise the prices on the products since costs were way over revenue. He expressed his extreme displeasure.

All my encounters earned me a visit from Bill who met me in Johannesburg where he told me that his bank, his accountant and his main buyer were all furious with me. I said I was not surprised since I had called them out on some terrible mistakes. He insisted I go with him to see his main buyer. I did not join the two in their discussion but, when Bill came out with a pack of papers, he said we should return to his hotel. There he laid out the papers which were invoices for products the firm had bought from him. As he looked at the papers, he suddenly began to realize that the buyer had been cheating him. I told Bill, "Now you know why all your business contacts here hate me."

I ended our meeting in Johannesburg by telling Bill that he had to cut costs and said the first one to cut was my services. I had reorganized his operation in Mozambique and obtained his foreign investment certificate. But did not want to get involved in his Johannesburg operation which was a mess.

I saw Bill a few times more when we were both in Johannesburg. Unfortunately, he had to sell his business in Mozambique for a fraction of what he had invested in it. He and his wife returned to the USA without ever living in their dream home on a small island in the Indian Ocean off the coast of Mozambique. Foreign investment is indeed a risky business. I won my spurs as a foreign investment advisor.

PUBLIC TO PRIVATE

My most memorable foreign investment experience was in
Turkey. While at our Consulate General in Monterrey,
Mexico I went to Washington for personal business, my
high school 30th anniversary reunion. While there I had
dinner with an old friend from Turkey with whom I had
worked several projects.

Ugurhan Tuncata was a remarkable man. I met him when
he came to the embassy to discuss using a new US
Government development program for a major undertaking
in Turkey, the building of a tunnel under the Bosporus
Strait to connect the railway from Europe that terminated
on the European side of the strait to the terminus of the
railway on the Asian side going through Turkey into the
Middle East, the old Hejaz Railway. The old dream of a
railway from Europe to Arabia.

He was working with an American firm, Parsons
Brinckerhoff, that was the granddaddy of underwater train
tunnels, its first being the one connecting the New York
Subway from Manhattan to Brooklyn. To get the project
started he wanted to tap into the new US Government fund
for money to do a feasibility study. The objective of the
fund was to provide seed money for projects in developing
countries that would produce significant trade

opportunities, another in a long line of US Government programs to combine the public and private sectors. The Bosporus Tunnel would do this in spades.

We got the money for the study, but it took many years to complete the project. The train tunnel under the Bosporus Strait, built by Tuncata's company, Gama, opened in 2013 but only for the trains of the Istanbul metro system. Plans are now underway to use it for freight trains headed to China.

While enormously wealthy, his company Gama, was and is the largest employer in Turkey outside the government, Urghan was not an impressive looking man. Short, wiry with a hair lip and a perennial twoday growth of beard he looked like a common laborer. But he was the genius who, with a couple of others of his engineering school classmates, built the largest civil engineering firm among Tukey's several giants in this field.

I recall Ur telling me about his first contract after graduating from engineering school. He bid, along with a number of other small construction firms, on the contract to build a small bridge in the remote mountains of southeast Turkey. He won the contract with an idea from his nimble mind. The largest cost for the project was the transport of cement to the job site. This was difficult terrain and the distance was long. Ur's bid came in far below the others.

The reason he was able to bid so low was he used the postal system itself to mail the cement to the job site. The postage for the heavy bags was far less than hiring a transportation firm to do the job. While he won that contract, the postal service made sure it did not get swamped by others following his lead by raising the postage on heavy packages way beyond the old prices.

This initial venture attested to Ur's ability to analyze an undertaking without restrictions and come up with truly innovative solutions. A brilliant mind and I always enjoyed exploring subjects with him.

Back to my dinner with Ur in Washington. We were discussing his latest business venture, a joint venture with the original public relations firm, Hill and Knowlton. I said I recalled Ur asking me about his daughter, who had just graduated from Princeton, taking a job with the US firm in its Washington office it had acquired, along with its founder Bob Gray.

Gray and Company had hit a gold mine working for the Reagan administration. It was the top influence peddler in the town at the time. Hill and Knowlton paid a wad to add this powerful PR firm to its stable. I told Ur that it would be an excellent start for his daughter who wanted to work in the world of politics. She went to work for Hill and Knowlton in DC.

Through his daughter Ur got to know the PR firm and decided to bring it into Turkey. I told him that it was the right time for starting a PR firm in the country. He then stopped me short by saying, "Leo I do not want your advice this time, I want you to run the company." I was stunned but recovered quickly and said, "If you can wait until next year when I can retire, I am your man." We agreed on my coming on board the following year.

I immediately went to the State Department's retirement office to make sure I could retire. I said I would be eligible to retire in June of the following year. The person I spoke to said, for system reasons, they retired people on the last day of the eligible month or the first of the next month. I replied, "Let's make for June 30."

After retirement I came back to Washington the next summer. After meeting all the people in the Washington office, including Mr. Gray, Ur insisted I go to New York City to meet the head office people.

The scene of my arrival was priceless. I showed up dressed, as was the custom at our consulate in Mexico, in a Stetson hat, hand tooled cowboy boots and a big silver buckle on my belt. The president of Hill and Knowlton did a double take but proceeded to talk about my new job.

I don't remember all of the conversation but do remember two things he told me. First, he said, "We don't think much of government employees."

I replied, "I am the Turks choice and they are the majority owners so we will both learn."

The president then asked, "Why did they pick you, when you have no public relations experience?"

I stopped him cold by saying, "I know how to sell to Turks, and you don't."

He then took me on a tour of the company's offices. I recall seeing lots of people working quietly in cubicles surrounded by higher ups sitting in offices with exterior windows. All were sneaking glances at me and I am sure muttering under their breath, "How did this complete novice get a prized post with the company, heading up one of our foreign operations, when they could have selected me." I suddenly realized that I and my Foreign Service colleagues had been guilty of the same envy whenever a political, not career, appointee arrived to head up our embassy. The shoe was definitely on the other foot.

I finally arrived at the new company in Ankara in September 1990. Ur was one of those few, wise Turks who knew that the big money in Turkey was in the government, not the business community in Istanbul. Thus, the office in Ankara, which was also the location of the headquarters of his Gama company.

I found that Ur had already established the office in a fancy new building located among several embassies. I inherited a staff consisting of an American from New York with substantial experience in public relations, three young Turks, recently graduated from Ankara's Middle East Technical University, an older Turk, retired from our embassy, with whom I had worked, a bodyguard/chauffer and a cleaning lady.

Ur had sunk considerable funds into setting up the new office. He had hired a very good staff, but lacked that vital element, he had no clients. In fact, he had left most of the job setting up the place to the American, who was a bit chary of me coming into takeover.

I discussed the situation with Ur and he agreed to carefully explain to the American that, while he appreciated his work in setting up the office, he had to understand that I was now in charge. He said he had spent a lot of money so far with nothing coming in. He gave me six months to make it work or he would close it down. I replied that I would be going at Christmas to join my wife and two daughters who by now were at our new embassy in Windhoek, Namibia. If I could get the company up and running, i.e. with clients and income, by then, I would come back. However, if I failed, I would simply stay in Namibia. In sum I had three months to turn Hill and Knowlton Turkey into a viable business. Ur agreed.

I then studied the business plan that the American specialist had brought from Hill and Knowlton. It called for beginning our work in Turkey by seeking clients among the US firms with operations in the country. My PR specialist had made a proposal to the US military installation near Ankara. They were having some labor problems and his offer was to counter the bad press the base was having with some positive stories, classic PR work. However, the installation was fiddling with an answer.

The specialist had also turned up an opportunity that involved a couple of US subsidiaries in Turkey. It seems there was a concern with solid waste pollution and the US firms involved were, along with the entire Turkish industry of plastic bottles and those who used them, faced with a stiff new tax on the plastic bottle which would have made them too expensive to use. A good opportunity but it was dragging on with no resolution.

The next stage was to offer services to all Turkish companies, using our services to the American subsidiaries as examples of what we could do. Finally, with our experience in the private sector we would offer our services to the Turkish government.

After reviewing the business plan I said no, we would do the reverse and start with the Turkish government. My main reason for this stemmed from the US parent having imposed on our office its rate structures used in the USA. I said the only potential client that would pay these hefty fees would be the government. Private firms could find several local options for PR work that were much less expensive.

I then made calls on my old contacts in Turkey. I was well received by my contacts at the Ministry of Foreign Affairs where we discussed Turkey's use of international PR firms to promote its entry into the European Union, a major piece of business. However, they explained that Hill and Knowlton refused to follow the guidelines when they bid on the contracts a year or two before. The Turks asked for a separate bid for each of three countries, the UK, France and Germany. Hill and Knowlton submitted one for all. We lost the bid.

I had experience with bidding on contracts from the side of looking for bids. As I always explained to potential bidders, they had to follow the bid specs exactly. I did not want reformulated specs. So, I immediately recognized Hill and Knowlton's mistake.

I emphasized to my Foreign Ministry friends that I was now in charge and they knew my work. They said yes, they wanted to work with me. They let me have a shot. They were not satisfied with the work being done by their PR firm in Germany and wanted me to submit a new bid for the PR work in Germany.

I also met with another good contact, the former head of the Turkish Union of Chambers of Commerce and Industry, with whom I had worked very closely when I was at the embassy ten years earlier. He was now the Minister of Information for the government, so I had the best contact one could have for doing PR work with the government. He greeted me with a warm welcome and fond memories of our work before. He asked what I thought of how far Turkey had come in the ten years since my departure. I told him all looked exactly as I had envisioned it when I was working hard to bring US investment to the country. Turkey had become the main manufacturing site in the Middle East and was busily shipping products to all of it neighbors. Turkish engineering and construction firms were working all over the Middle East, Africa and Central Asia. And of course, we now had the new Turkish aircraft factory building the latest planes under license to General Dynamics.

I told my friend to give me a pencil and paper and I would write down what Turkey would be like in another ten years which he could keep in his desk to open in ten years. In sum I once more showed him my confidence in Turkey and where it was going. He urged me to call on him whenever he could be of assistance. I said I was sure I would be contacting him.

GULF WAR

I was to start by rebidding on the PR work for the Foreign Ministry in Germany when the winds of war drastically altered my plans. I got to Turkey just after the Iraqi's had invaded Kuwait and seized the country. The invasion and subsequent war to oust the Iraqis became the major issue. The invasion and seizure spilled over into Turkey in the form of border tensions with its southern neighbor and the revival of an ultra-leftwing group called Dev Gench that was going around killing two kinds of people, Turkish military officers and American businessmen.

That last note was chilling for the entire community of American businessmen of which I was a highly visible member. Our periodic meetings with the US Embassy, which featured me on the opposite side of the table from the current Commercial Attache and my former staff from when I held the same position ten years before, were dominated by talk of assassination. We all took precautions.

For my part I hardened my suite of offices located on the ground floor of a very modern apartment building. I had special plastic reinforcement covers placed on our windows designed to hold the glass if a bomb was set off near-by. I imposed one firm command, no one was to be admitted into the office unless he had an appointment with one of us. I said I didn't care if it was your mother outside calling you, no entry unless it had been prearranged. I also spent time with my bodyguard come chauffer reviewing our security. As a former member of the Kurdish guerilla forces in southern and eastern Turkey he was a real veteran of guerilla warfare.

Fortunately, I was not targeted by the Dev Gench but I knew of two of my associates who had been. The method used was to force entry into a company's offices, take the American head into one office and leave the Turkish staff tied up in another. After a while a shot or two would announce that the American was dispatched and the perpetrators would leave with the Turks still tied up.

Another problem was that the building, in which our offices were housed, was a well-known residence for Iraqis living in Ankara. So, it was also a target for Kuwaiti retaliation for the invasion of their home country. From my office window I could see the Iraq and Saudi Arabian embassies facing each other across a street. I kept an eye out for demonstrations flaring up there.

WEAPONS OF MASS DESTRUCTION

One evening I was at the small US Air Force installation in Ankara where I was watching the news program "60 Minutes."   It proceeded to show Russian satellite photos, that had been enhanced by a studio in London, of a small mountain in Iraq in which the Iraqis were enriching uranium for nuclear weapons. I took one look and said, "Where did this crap come from?"

There was no way the Iraqis could be enriching uranium and certainly not enough for nuclear weapons, they did not have the funds nor the talent to do this job. At the time there were only four sites in all the world where uranium could be enriched for weapons, two in the USA, one in the USSR and one in France. The fifth was certainly not in Iraq.

I subsequently went to New York City to consult with the head office about a major bid we were making. While there I talked to the company's video people about the video I had seen on "60 Minutes." They said there was such a demand for news from the 24 hour a day TV news programs any well-made video would get aired. They also said that "60 Minutes" main supplier for news was the US government itself.

At that time the USA and several other major countries, as well as the UN, had demanded that the Iraqis leave Kuwait. The pressure was intense and soon practically all the world was calling for Iraq's withdrawal. In spite of all the world calling for Iraq to withdraw, the US Congress was debating a declaration of war. Our Washington office got a $10 million contract from the "Citizens to Free Kuwait," a front set up by the Kuwaiti Embassy in Washington, to cajole our Congress into declaring war. I finally realized that the video I had discussed with Hill and Knowlton's video team in New York had been made by those very same people. It was part of our campaign to press the Congress to act. We used the video as evidence the Iraqis had, drum roll please, "Weapons of Mass Destruction."

Congress declared war. The US led a massive coalition of forces to invade Iraq and totally annihilate the Iraqi military in a matter of days. Needless to say, the Iraqis in Kuwait went flying back to Iraq, leaving Kuwait "liberated" by the USA.

About a year later I was in Washington where all the news was about a Kuwaiti woman who had appeared before a Congressional committee during the build up to the Gulf War, telling tales of Iraqi soldiers atrocities, the most horrendous one being stripping babies from incubators for hospitals in Iraq. Both that horrible story and the "weapons of mass destruction," proved to be wrong, our forces found no nuclear weapons or any Iraq uranium enrichment facilities. But they were major planks in the wall of outrage demanding war with Iraq.

Well guess what? My company Hill and Knowlton had provided the Kuwaiti Congressional witness and tales of "weapons of mass destruction" based on the video I had seen on "60 Minutes."   My friends asked if I was embarrassed to have been working for the company that had used such deceit? By then I had moved on from Hill and Knowlton. I responded by saying, "we got a $10 million contract to get the US to go to war with Iraq. We got the whole world to go to war with Iraq. We earned our money fair and square."

SUCCESS

During the height of the war next door in Iraq I found that the New York office of Hill and Knowlton was negotiating a contract to provide PR services to the Turkish government to offset the bad press for tourism coming from the war next door in Iraq. I told Ur that, if Hill and Knowlton wanted to do any business in Turkey, it had to go through me, or I was leaving. He called the New York office and got them to let me handle the matter.

I knew the New York crowd wanted to give me enough rope to hang myself. They didn't think I could do the job. Their poor image of me was emphasized by their regional manager in London who came to see what we were doing. He announced to me and my entire staff that we would never get the tourism contract. I said we would see.

I pulled out all the stops in pursuit of the contract. Ur found through his extensive contacts that the government had earmarked $2.5 million for the contract to counter the bad tourism image Turkey was suffering due to chaos in Iraq. We knew how much to bid. I had learned in my government service that governments set budgets for contracts. The trick for those bidding on the contract is to cost your bid as close to the money allocated as possible. In other words, bidding on a government contract is not an open-ended thing, there is a set budget. Of course, one has to provide the services expected with your bid, but, "salvaging Turkish tourism," was a pretty nebulous goal. The only obligatory service we had was to place a video praising Turkish tourism on CNN. The Turks wanted this since the Greeks had already done one.

Right in line with my plan we got the contact for $2.5 million from the Turkish government on Dec 10. The entire Hill and Knowlton company from New York to London applauded my work. The president of the company came to Turkey to officially congratulate me and my team. The company raised my pay by 50%. I was their new star. As agreed with Ur, I left to join my family in Windhoek for Christmas agreeing to come back in the New Year.

VISUAL POLLUTION

On return from Christmas leave I did clear up one other matter. My American specialist had left the firm and returned to the USA. He had left one project with one of our young Turks to finish, the proposal for solving Turkey's "solid waste pollution" problem. I reviewed the work she had done with our American specialist and found that they had missed the actual problem involved.

The problem was concentrated in the towns on Turkey's southwest coast which were enjoying a boon in the tourism business. This is where the Mediterranean meets the Aegean Sea and is blessed with fine beaches and a wealth of historic sites. First among these is the town of Bodrum which was the ancient Halicarnassus, the home of Herodotus, the "father of history," and one of the Seven Wonders of the World, the tomb of King Mausolus, now known as the "Mausoleum of Halicarnassus." You can actually see a replica of the wonder in New York City, the tomb of President U.S. Grant.

The Mediterranean climate features hot, dry summers followed by heavy, often torrential, autumn rains. During the summer the trash and garbage would pile-up in Bodrum and the other towns and then be carried off to sea by the autumn rains leaving the rubbish to sink to the sea bottom.

Bodrum and the other coastal towns had fleets of glass bottom boats taking tourists to see the ancient Greek boats that had sunk to the sea bottom. However, while the tourists did see old sunken boats, instead of amphoras of oil and other ancient cargo, the boats were sprinkled with plastic bottles blaring labels such as Coca-Cola, Clorox, Tide and other commercial labels. I told my young colleague, "What we have here is visual pollution, not solid waste pollution."

We devised a plan to set up large collection containers for plastic bottles, station these around the town and promote using the containers. A much less expensive and disrupting solution than taxing the plastic bottle out of use.

Before we had a chance to proffer our solution to the new organization of plastic bottle makers and users, set up to answer the government's challenge, my young colleague came to me one morning and said the new organization had sent us their plan to solve the problem. More importantly, they were to have a meeting that very day in Istanbul to decide how to go forward. We went immediately to the airport and flew to Istanbul. I read the new plan, which was in Turkish, while flying, stretching my modest command of the language to the max to capture the salient points of the plan.

We arrived a bit late to the meeting but quickly got into the discussion of the proposal, which was dramatically different from ours, and still relied on a tax on the bottles. When the discussion got to me, I dramatically tossed the plan on the table in front of all and said, "If what I am hearing is what you want to do, it is not in this proposal." The room hushed and my young Turkish colleague looked like she wanted to slide under the table since she was the only other person in the room that knew that I had only just read the plan with my limited command of the language. After a painful silence the others in the room began to say, "you are right, this plan does not do what we want." I then said we had a plan to propose if they wanted and all agreed to hold off a decision until we submitted our plan.

I would like to say that we got the contract, but we did not. The work went to a Turkish firm that was substantially cheaper than were we. But the plan adopted did follow our suggestion to use better collection of the plastic bottles instead of taxes to cure the problem.

ADIOS

I came back in the new year set on making our proposal to the Foreign Ministry to do their PR work in Germany for entering the EU. My first move was to contact Hill and Knowlton Germany to ask for a copy of their proposal, which had been part of Hill and Knowlton's overall proposal in the previous bidding. They sent me a copy, in German. I replied that no one in our shop spoke German so would they please send a copy in English. That request earned me a visit from Ur who came to tell me that the home office in New York had called him to tell us to not demand work from its office in Germany.

I explained what I had done and that I had hoped there would be better cooperation among Hill and Knowlton's foreign subsidiaries. Ur said we had to follow company policies. I reminded him that I had done the impossible in winning the tourism contract and knew what had to be done to get the Foreign Ministry contract. Of course, the actual work would have to be done in Germany, but I was the only way Hill and Knowlton would get this lucrative contract. If I could not handle it as I did with the tourism contract, I would not be successful and, since I knew he had short patience for failed work, I preferred to not be involved. I stayed for a while longer basically reporting on the work we did for the government on the tourism campaign but left the company a few months later.

What I did not understand was Ur's real plan. It became obvious that he wanted the company to be a success, not to stay in the business, but to sell his share back to Hill and Knowlton for a fast profit. I had delivered what he needed and was no longer useful to the plan.

A truly incredible experience. There I was, after spending 25 years in government service advising American firms on how to do business in Bongo Bongo and Pango Pango, faced with having to actually make a new business work. I was the most surprised person when we got the big contract, since I knew exactly what I had done to get the job.   The most satisfying result was to realize that I had not been blowing smoke over those many years, my advice and ideas really worked. I actually used them to make a new enterprise work. The experience confirmed the validity of my advice to others and confirmed my ability as an actual businessman.

Two new notches in my gun, entrepreneur and "spin doctor." I always tell people I wish my first job had been as a "spin doctor" since I learned so much about basic motivation and how to influence people that would have served me well in any number of careers.

TRADE CENTER

Perhaps the most traditional job I had in promoting the global economy was to set up a foreign investment for a South African company in the USA. I came back from our stay in Namibia with an agreement to set up a new venture in Orlando, Florida for a business contact I had in Johannesburg. The idea was rather straight forward, the bans on South African exports to the USA had been lifted with the end of Apartheid. The stage was set for companies there to start selling to the USA. However, most of the exporters' relationships and contacts were gone so they had to set up shop all-over again.

My South African contact was planning to build the "South African Trade Center" at the airport in Orlando. The center would offer offices, show room facilities, and warehouse storage at one site almost next to the runway at the airport.

Since my wife was being transferred to New York City, I knew that I would not be able to spend all my time in Orlando so convinced my brother, who by then was a retired US Air Force Officer living east of Tampa and not far from Orlando, to join me in the venture. Between the two we would set up and manage the new business.

I arrived in Orlando with two contacts my South African owner had made, one, a warehouse under construction at the airport and the other a building already in place that had been built as an exhibit hall. The building being built would require a substantial amount of money to install the trade center while the existing building could be converted to our purposes for far less money. I convinced the owner to choose the latter option and negotiated a contract to use the facility for three months at no cost, thus allowing us to see what would happen, without a possible major loss.

My brother and I then set up an office in the exhibit hall that served as our operations center and show office for prospective clients, i.e. South African companies that needed an office in the USA to handle their exports to the country. The center had a readymade warehouse since the exhibit hall had a large storage facility built into the structure. We left the exhibit area open, since each client would have different requirements for showing his wares, so we would custom make these.

We worked a few weeks for costs, i.e. commuting from Tampa for my brother and accommodation and transportation for me. We were set when the owner contacted us from South Africa to say that sales of the facility were not going well and he could no longer afford to pay us our expenses. I offered to continue with the project for a share of the business. He agreed and we proceeded.

I was not sure why he was having trouble selling the center. While the idea of having a platform in the US for your exports to the country was a valid reason for using it, there was another, less obvious reason to open an office and other facilities in the USA. South Africa had tough regulations for obtaining foreign exchange. One easy way to get the foreign exchange was to pay costs associated with exporting your goods. Thus the Trade Center was a strong draw just to get access to foreign exchange.

No matter how good the offer was, the owner in Johannesburg was not able to find sufficient clients to merit opening the center. He asked me if there were companies in the US that would be interested. I looked around and found a company in Orlando, owned by South Africans, that was interested in the trade center idea. I passed on their interest to my man in Johannesburg. But in the end the two sides could not come to an agreement, so we had to close the center before it actually opened.

Fortunately, since we had no expense for the building, the owner did not lose much. My brother was another issue. He asked me who was going to pay him for his work? I replied, "Welcome to the world of being in business for yourself." I also advised him to not go into business.

Add Trade Center Manager to my resume.

BENEFITS OF GLOBAL ECONOMY

The tales I tell about my work in and with the global economy are the stuff of this book. However, I would be remiss to not talk about the benefits of the global economy. First and foremost, the global economy allows participants to grow beyond what their homelands would permit, it provides a world market. It also goes a long way to rationalizing production around the world, basically allowing countries to engage in what they do best, while exchanging goods for items better left to other makers.

ECONOMIC DEVELOPMENT

We have now seen how the global economy has provided the best mechanism yet found for poor countries to advance up the economic ladder. The only way for less developed countries to grow is through transfers of wealth from the rich to the poor.

Much is made of governments providing such transfers in the form of "Official Development Assistance" or ODA. These are the loans and grants given by rich countries to their poorer relatives. However, this is not enough to truly raise the poor countries to the next level. At present the total for the year is about $150 billion. Compare this to the total world economic output of about $ 80 trillion dollars a year and one sees that it is a mere drop in the bucket. There have been several massive transfers of wealth between nations over the centuries. One can speak of the Mongol conquest of China that resulted in massive flows of wealth from China to Mongolia that was probably offset by massive migration of Mongols to China. Another was the Spanish conquests in the Americas which gained a mountain of gold and silver for Spain.

There have been two massive transfers of wealth from rich to poor nations in recent history. The first occurring in the petroleum trade. In the 1970s the major oil exporting nations, read Iran, Saudi Arabia, Kuwait, the UAE and Nigeria took back the concessions they had sold to the major oil producing companies. However, nothing really changed in the industry, the companies continued to produce the oil and deliver it to the world. The only change was that the price of the oil sold was set by the producing countries themselves, not the companies. They had even created the Organization of Petroleum Exporting Countries as a mechanism to control production and thus the price.

Oil has a very inelastic demand, i.e. as supply goes down, price goes up since we will pay practically any price for it.

To gain some understanding of how inelastic demand for oil is, we pay about $3 a gallon for gasoline in the USA. In England the price is $7-8 and in Italy even higher. In other words, we will drive our cars no matter how high the price of gasoline

OPEC members understood this and set about to set prices by setting supply. The important thing to understand here is that sovereign nations can collude to set prices, but private companies may not. The reference case here was the US Court decision that led to the breakup of the largest company in the world, Standard Oil (ESSO), owned by the richest man in America, John D. Rockefeller. That was an anti-trust case and not exactly a collusion charge, but the intent is the same, to not allow anyone to control the market, since we are a market-based economy and an open market is essential to our economic success. Similar laws are in place throughout the world.

The result of the OPEC nations gaining control over supply and pricing was rapid, oil prices shot up like a rocket. A barrel of oil produced in Saudi Arabia at about 25 cents was priced at $25 by the government. A curious result, however, is that, while the OPEC nations were reaping huge increases in revenue, the oil companies were making record profits. In effect the seizure of the concessions was a "win-win" deal for both sides.

Now what did this mean for economic development? Well the OPEC nations represented relatively poor nations, Saudi Arabia, Iran, Kuwait, Bahrain, the UAE, Nigeria, and Ecuador. I leave out Venezuela since it was at the time the wealthiest nation in South America. The windfall rise in prices meant massive transfers of wealth from the importing countries, mainly the rich countries, to these relatively poor nations.

I recall sitting in a meeting at the State Department listening to a colleague who was an "Arabist," or expert on the Arab world talking about how these simple Bedouins would not be able to spend so much money, thus acting as a drag on the world economy. I countered that I was sure they would find ways to spend the money, if not for goods and services, then as loans to others. Kuwait was already receiving most of its national income from interest payments on loans. In the event the exporting nations learned very fast how to use their new-found riches. Saudi Arabia even had to resort to borrowing to keep up their new pace of spending.

The second recent massive increase in transfers of wealth from the rich to the poor nations comes from the global economy, with China being the best example. Here we have what was formerly the largest poor nation on the earth now advanced to being the second largest economy in the world. China's route to riches runs directly through the global economy. Its exports around the world have provided it with the massive amounts of funds for domestic investment.

To gain some insight into how the global economy outpaces ODA in helping poor nations rise up the ranks, China runs trade surpluses with both the USA and the EU of some $300-500 billion a year. Compare this to the $150 billion in ODA each year. China is getting up to one trillion dollars in massive transfers of wealth each year. When one understands this, he understands how a very poor country has become the second largest economy in the world.

And China is by no means alone in this favorable development. There is a constant flow of formerly poor countries joining the ranks of the better off via engaging with the global economy, here one thinks of India, Indonesia, South Korea, Taiwan, Brazil, Russia, and more.

In sum, the global economy has been the most important means yet devised to provide economic development to poor nations.

CONSUMER

Another major beneficiary of the global economy is the consumer. As I stated at the beginning, the basic motivation for the global economy is the consumer's constant search for the best product at the best price. The global economy allows the consumer to source the whole world for his needs. In doing so he maximizes the purchasing power of his purse.

I use my shirt as an example of this result. Via the global economy I am able to buy three shirts for the price of one if left to only buy in my own economy. This simple equation sums up the demand factor for the global economy.

INFLATION

In classic textbook economics there are two types of inflation, cost push and demand pull. Cost push means as the cost of production go up the price of the product must increase. Demand pull is that when demand exceeds supply the price of the product will go up until demand tapers off. The best recent example of this was the housing "bubble" of the first decade of the new millennium, when housing prices reached a certain level the demand began to fall.

I would add two other inflationary pressures, credit and insurance. Easy to see the effect of credit. Easy to obtain mortgages fueled the housing "bubble" of a decade ago. Another example is the widespread availability of student loans which resulted in major increases in the cost of college education. Insurance is less obvious but look at two examples. Auto insurance has allowed auto repair shops to raise their prices to exorbitant levels. Likewise, health insurance has induced quantum increase in the cost of health care which now takes almost one-fifth of the entire economy. The underlying consideration here is that one doesn't really care about the cost of the service as long as someone else is paying.

No matter what the cause for inflation, the global economy offers a very effective control on it. When the price of a good or service rises too high, one can import a cheaper substitute from abroad. A good case could be made that the amazing increase in US imports from China over the last decade or so put a limit on inflation. Inflation during the rapid rise in US imports from China was practically non-existent.

WORLD PEACE

Perhaps the most vital result of the global economy is its contribution to world peace. Following the Second World War there developed a concept that nations that trade and have commercial intercourse with each other would be less willing to wage war on its partners. This was the basis for forming what is now the European Union.

As the global economy grows, so too does it give more reason to avoid confrontation. Perhaps the global economy will be the instrument through which we achieve that highest of all goals, world peace.